BIBLICAL HERMENEUTICS

An Introduction

Duncan S. Ferguson

John Knox Press
ATLANTA

Library of Congress Cataloging-in-Publication Data

Ferguson, Duncan S. (Duncan Sheldon), 1937–
Biblical hermeneutics.

Bibliography: p.
Includes index.
1. Bible—Hermeneutics. I. Title.
BS476.F45 1986 220.6′01 85-45456
ISBN 0-8042-0050-5

10 9 8 7 6 5 4 3 2 1
Printed in the United States of America
John Knox Press
Atlanta, Georgia 30365

Preface

The inspiration for this study grew out of the reflection that the Christian faith has been so variously understood over the centuries by so many well-meaning and scholarly people. Why is it that sincere persons, eager to be true to the self-disclosure of God, differ so widely on what they believe this revelation to be and mean? The Apostle's statement, "Now we see in a mirror dimly" (1 Cor. 13:12), certainly seems accurate.

In this study, I attempt to examine why it is we do not see more clearly and how it may be possible to read the biblical documents which testify to God's self-disclosure with a better chance of discerning their meaning. This hermeneutical responsibility will not go away if we believe God's Word has ever been spoken to the human family. The interpreter must account for any blurred vision in the attempt to make the Word attested to in Scripture speak with poignancy and force to a world starving for some authentic utterance from God. How is it possible for God's self-disclosure, hidden as it is behind the barriers of time, language, and culture, to leap forward into our contemporary situation and give us values, guidance, and comfort?

This theme has been developed in three major sections. In Section I, there is an attempt to establish some starting points, including a definition of the task of hermeneutics, a clarification of the current issues in the debate, and a discussion of the critical assumptions which must be clear to the interpreter in order to proceed to the hermeneutical task. Section II endeavors to provide some hermeneutical guidelines and practical approaches for contemporary interpreters of the Christian faith who use the Bible as their primary resource. Section III is an application of the theme to various interpreters of the Christian faith across the centuries of church history. Each figure in these case studies has been selected because that person represents a major strand of Christian thought. The final chapter suggests some ways the Bible might be best used to guide the church.

I am indebted to several people who encouraged and assisted me in this project. John McIntyre of New College, University of Edinburgh, put me up to it originally and gently pointed the way. The good people of Whitworth College granted me a sabbatical which allowed me some concentrated time. James I. McCord of Princeton Theological Seminary provided me with an appointment as a Visiting Fellow of the Seminary, making available invaluable resources. My former colleagues in the Department of Religion and Philosophy at Whitworth have read bits and pieces of the manuscript and made excellent suggestions for improvement. Tom Gillespie, Herman Waetjen, David Hubbard, and Lewis Mudge, a quartet of enormous erudition, lent their support. And, of course, the superb staff of John Knox Press have been extremely helpful. Finally, I'm grateful to my family. My wife Dorothy's love and patience were indispensable, and my son Brian's requests to play soccer in mid-paragraph and our cocker spaniel Riley's rearranging of the manuscript kept the project in perspective.

Contents

DEDICATION

Dedicated to Edward B. Lindaman, warm friend, visionary Christian, and inspirational leader.

I

The Issues of Biblical Hermeneutics

Before one assumes the important responsibility of interpreting Scripture, it is important to understand the complex issues associated with the task. This section introduces the reader to several of these issues and suggests that faith and historical study are the prerequisites for an adequate hermeneutical system.

1

Hermeneutics: The Continuing Responsibility

The Complexity and Urgency of the Task

In the last several decades, hermeneutics has moved to the forefront of the theological discussion. Today it continues to be a prime concern for all who endeavor to understand the Christian faith. Of particular concern is the way in which the Bible functions as the source of our knowledge about God and God's self-disclosure in Jesus Christ. If in fact the Bible is our primary resource for such knowledge, the interpretation of the Bible takes on extraordinary importance in the life of the church. The purpose of this volume is to assist those who want to better understand the Bible as the primary resource for discerning the will of God for human life.

It is ironic that Christians cannot seem to agree on how the Bible can best be understood, though virtually as one, they believe the Bible to be the key that unlocks the mystery of God's way. This irony is rooted in the fact that the church of Christ, divided as it is into an almost limitless variety of confessions and denominations, has at least this one common element—the Bible. Given this shared loyalty it would seem that there should be a great deal more commonality of interpretation. Certainly, as the branches of the church come together seeking unity it is their common hope that the widespread acceptance of biblical authority will provide the basis for agreement.

Strange as it may appear to the external observer, though, Christians cannot agree on the meaning of biblical authority, let alone on a common interpretation of Scripture. Conflict over the Bible cuts right across most denominational differences. This struggle, as alive today as ever, is often divisive and harmful to the ongoing life of the church. There is, however, a positive side to the debate; the struggle has produced a vast literature and invaluable perspectives that have added to the wealth of all Christians. If ways can be found to minimize the destructive aspects of the debate the conversation may continue to produce positive enrichment for the church. It is hoped that these pages will make a positive contribution toward this end.

The first order of business with this goal in mind, then, is to define hermeneutical responsibility. This chapter is an attempt to clarify the commission to interpret the Scriptures in a way which both is faithful to their original intention and guides the church today in fulfilling its mission to the world.

Toward a Definition of Hermeneutics

Hermeneutics has been traditionally defined as the *study of the locus and principles of interpretation*—particularly as it is applied to the interpretation of ancient texts. Though valid, this definition needs amplification and qualification since there has been a steady shifting of emphases in carrying out the hermeneutical task, especially since the Reformation. The Roman Catholic assertion that the revelation testified to in Scripture can only be understood in light of the tradition presented by the church, which became for the Catholics a partial solution to the hermeneutical problem, was rejected by the Reformers. Against this view of tradition the Reformers posited the doctrine of *sola scriptura,* maintaining that Scripture has its *own* illuminating power. This became one important aspect of the hermeneutical position of the Reformation, though the implications of it may not have been fully understood by the Reformers or their immediate followers.[1]

Following the Reformation, Protestant hermeneutics dealt primarily with the rules to be observed in exegesis. In Protestant Orthodoxy, because of the identification of Scripture as the Word of God, the hermeneutical problem was focused on the study of each biblical document, both the literary context and the wider situation in which it appeared. This tendency was given further impetus by the rise of critical biblical scholarship in the nineteenth century. Understanding Scripture required the study of (1) the structure and idioms of biblical language, (2) the type of literature represented, i.e., prose or poetry, history or allegory, literal or symbolic, or perhaps a particular genre found in the Bible, such as apocalyptic, (3) the historical background, (4) the geographical conditions, and (5) the life setting (*Sitz im Leben*).[2] This hermeneutical tradition, with few but very important exceptions, continues in full sway into our own century.

These important exceptions, raised most noticeably by Friedrich Schleiermacher and Wilhelm Dilthey, have greatly influenced the development of hermeneutics in our own time, especially the work of a modern leader in the field—Rudolf Bultmann. Following the tradition of Schleiermacher and Dilthey, the word "hermeneutics" has taken on a much broader reference due largely to Bultmann. It is generally used to describe the attempt to span the gap between past and present—a gap not only temporal but also cultural, dealing with world views and ways of thinking. In the case of biblical hermeneutics it is a jump from the agrarian world in which the redemptive events occurred and were recorded to an industrial or even post-industrial world in which we read the record and live in faith.[3]

Carl Braaten defines hermeneutics as "the science of reflecting on how a word or an event in a past time and culture may be understood and become existentially meaningful in our present situation."[4] It involves "both the methodological rules to be applied in exegesis as well as the epistemological presuppositions of historical understanding."[5] James Robinson, among others, describes this wider reference of hermeneutics as a shift from "explaining" (*Erklarung*) to "understanding" (*Verstehen*).[6] It is in this broader sense that the plural term *hermeneutics* is generally used. The singular, *hermeneutic*, is most frequently used to refer to a particular frame of reference from which to proceed to interpretation. A given hermeneutic is essentially a self-consciously chosen starting point containing certain ideological, attitudinal, and methodological components designed to aid the work of interpretation and facilitate maximum understanding.

More recently emphasis has shifted again, due in large measure to the work of Hans-Georg Gadamer and Paul Ricoeur. Gadamer, in his book *Truth and Method*, argues that the hermeneutical task should go beyond the scientific investigation of the text in an attempt to gain "truth." According to Gadamer hermeneutics is concerned to seek the experience of truth that transcends the sphere of the control of the scientific method. Paul Ricoeur shares Gadamer's view that the hermeneutical question is the primary philosophical question. He focuses his attention on what has become the overriding issue of philosophers in the twentieth century—the philosophy of language. Language is revelatory and the interpreter must assume the posture of "second naïveté" or "willed naïveté," allowing the text to reveal and enlighten. Both Gadamer and Ricoeur agree that what is at stake in exercising hermeneutical responsibility is more than the interpretation of an ancient text; it involves the probing of the mysteries of ultimate reality through language.

Thus the word *hermeneutics* has a rich and varied history; it should be understood primarily as the task of "hearing" what an ancient text has to say. The simple definition, the rules and principles of interpretation, still holds, but it must be placed in the context of its shifting meanings, with emphasis placed on allowing the past to inform the present and point to the future.

The Role of Preunderstanding

The term *preunderstanding* describes the phenomenon of perspective which the observer of any event brings to its meaning. This term is chosen because it is comprehensive and includes within its scope a number of other words and phrases which have a similar but on occasion slightly different and more specific and limited meaning. *Preunderstanding* may be defined as *a body of assumptions and attitudes which a person brings to the perception and interpretation of reality or any aspect of it.*

Whenever anyone attempts to "hear" what the text has to say, that person inevitably hears and identifies the sounds from within a prior structure of experiences or preunderstanding. To doubt one's own capacity to be free from preunderstanding which necessarily colors the perceptions and interpretations of reality is the beginning of epistemological wisdom.[7] None may claim an "Archimedean vantage point" from which to peer at truth. C. S. Lewis makes the point by describing what happens when a human being encounters a strange creature on a foreign planet:

> It was only many days later that Ransom discovered how to deal with these sudden losses of confidence. They arose when the rationality of the *hross* tempted you to think of it as a man. Then it became abominable—a man seven feet high, with a snaky body, covered, face and all, with thick black animal hair, and whiskered like a cat. But starting from the other end you had an animal with everything an animal ought to have—glossy coat, liquid eye, sweet breath and whitest teeth—and added to all these, as though paradise had never been lost and earliest dreams were true, the charm of speech and reason. Nothing could be more disgusting than the one impression; nothing more delightful than the other. It all depended on the point of view.[8]

One's point of view makes a significant difference. Indeed, it would appear that nearly all perception and subsequent understanding and interpretation of reality proceed in some measure from the preunderstanding of the participant.

In nearly every quarter where knowledge is pursued in a serious and disciplined manner there is a recognition that the preunderstanding of the observer enters into his or her apprehension of reality. The pursuit of universal knowledge of things as they are in themselves, while still a worthy objective, is generally accepted as an extraordinarily difficult task. Almost all knowledge is conditioned in some measure by the assumptions and attitudes of the knower.

The social sciences have helped us to understand how much of our background we bring to our truth-seeking. Psychology and sociology have taught us that we are beings whose rational comprehension is contingent on emotional states and social conditioning. Our intelligence, shaped as it is by sensation, interest, and feeling, gives less than true form and structure to sense-experience. The influence of our environment affects the form we give to the world around us.

The political scientist and the economist are also concerned with the influences of preunderstanding. H. Richard Niebuhr gives the example of their careful scrutiny of noble phrases such as "the natural rights of man," "all men are created equal," "inalienable rights," etc., to see if they may not be historically conditioned.[9] One does not need to be a professional economist or political scientist to recognize that such phrases are more the product of prior assumptions than of any objective statement of empirical fact. They may, as the

Marxist asserts, be mere rationalizations for human activity which have economic considerations as their motive. Whatever the case, the point is made that the environmentally conditioned preunderstanding of the observer must always be taken into account. No observer can get into a realm beyond space and time to give an account of the way the world really is.

Historians, too, have been quick to acknowledge different forms of preunderstanding in their work. That history is always understood and written from some point of view is generally accepted by most modern historians.[10] That even the very selection of material is in large part determined by one's preunderstanding and intentions has been acknowledged in one manual on historical research:

> Since guiding ideas affect both search and selection, let us call the researcher's temperament (i.e., the whole temperament of his mind) and his present intentions and hypotheses his total interest. We may then say without implying any blame that his interests will determine his discoveries, his selection, his pattern making, and his presentation.[11]

Preunderstanding has long been regarded among philosophers as a factor in perception, and the debate as to its influence continues today. Something akin to preunderstanding is recognized by Immanuel Kant when he insists in *The Critique of Pure Reason* that we have no certain knowledge of things in themselves but that our mind gives them shape. Kant argues that our mind conditions objects by means of unifying principles (e.g., time and space) and that in a sense a mind constitutes reality. He goes on to explain that

> . . . although all our cognition begins with experience . . . all does not precisely spring up out of experience. For it may easily happen that even our empirical cognition may be a compound of that which we have received through our impressions, and of that which our proper cognition-faculty . . . supplies from itself.[12]

The role of preunderstanding in the perception and formulation of reality has also been acknowledged in the existential-ontological philosophy of Martin Heidegger. In discussing the ontological structure of human existence, Heidegger says that "understanding always touches on the whole constitution of being in the world."[13] Magda

King, commenting on this Heideggerian theme, writes, "Meaning does not lie in words, or in things, but in the remarkable structure of our understanding itself. We move in advance in a *horizon of understanding* from which and in reference to which the things we meet are intelligible to us."[14]

A slightly different approach to the theme of preunderstanding is developed in the tradition of linguistic analysis by Donald D. Evans. He is concerned to show in what ways human utterances are logically connected with practical commitments, attitudes, and feelings. More specifically, he attempts to provide a logic for adequately dealing with God's self-disclosure which demands by its very nature an appropriate preunderstanding if we are to apprehend it. After a detailed description of the self-involving elements in everyday language, he applies this "logic of self-involvement" to the biblical doctrine of creation. For example, Evans refers to what he calls an "onlook," which is a comprehensive term used to describe the "core of many attitudes."[15] Applying the notion of onlook to creation he writes, "the recognition of God's glory in world-Creation depends on the onlook which a man adopts."[16] In other words, one needs a certain type of preunderstanding (a parabolic onlook) to grasp the significance of the doctrine of creation (a complex parable).

Even scientists, whose very method is designed to exclude the intrusion of the personal dimension, have acknowledged the presence of preunderstanding. Since Einstein, many authors have agreed with Philipp Frank that the theory of relativity "proposes a new view of space and time and brings the observing scientist himself into the picture of the physical world."[17] One well-known scientist turned philosopher, Michael Polanyi, has devoted his energies in recent years to formulating a theory of personal knowledge suited for science. He observes: "We must learn to accept as our ideal a knowledge that is manifestly personal."[18]

Epistemologists sometimes distinguish between knowledge that is recognitive (for example, recognizing a friend) and knowledge that is cognitive (for example, knowing a proposition is true). Polanyi's efforts have been directed toward diminishing if not contradicting this distinction. For Polanyi recognition is essential to all acts of knowing. In *The Tacit Dimension* he states:

> The declared aim of modern science is to establish a strictly detached, objective knowledge. Any falling short of this ideal is accepted only as a temporary imperfection, which we must aim at eliminating. But suppose that tacit thought forms an indispensable part of all knowledge, then the ideal of eliminating all personal elements of knowledge would, in effect, aim at the destruction of all knowledge.[19]

Polanyi's most systematic analysis of the personal dimension in all knowledge is found in his Gifford Lectures entitled *Personal Knowledge* in which he argues that human beings must always make commitments and assume responsibility in the quest for knowledge. He writes:

> As I acknowledge, in reflecting on the process of discovery, the gap between the evidence and the conclusions which I draw from them, and account for my bridging of this gap in terms of my personal responsibility, so also will I acknowledge that in childhood I have formed my most fundamental beliefs by exercising my native intelligence within the social milieu of a particular place and time. I shall submit to this fact as defining the condition within which I am called upon to exercise my responsibility.[20]

In the field of theology, the interest in preunderstanding has centered in hermeneutics. Here the work of Rudolf Bultmann is most influential. "Every interpretation," he notes, "incorporates a particular prior understanding."[21] Again he says: "It will be clear that every interpreter brings with him certain conceptions, perhaps idealistic or psychological, as presuppositions of his exegesis, in most cases unconsciously."[22] In one essay he asks the pointed question, "Is presuppositionless exegesis possible?" to which he replies in some detail both yes and no. The "yes," however, refers to the possibility of doing exegesis without presupposing the results, whereas the "no" acknowledges that every exegete approaches the text with specific questions and a certain idea of the subject matter with which the text is concerned.[23] For Bultmann preunderstanding (*Vorverständnis*) is not only an ever present factor to be accounted for, it is also necessary to the task of interpretation. Without it, understanding would not be possible at all. For as Günther Bornkamm points out in referring to Bultmann's use of the term,

> Only the bearing of life on relevant matters that makes itself felt in preunderstanding can establish communication between the text and the interpreter and make possible a proper examination of the text, allowing the interpreter to ask himself about the text and to revise it on the basis of his own self-understanding.[24]

It is evident that some form of preunderstanding is generally recognized as an omnipresent feature in the apprehension and interpretation of reality. We peer at the world through colored glasses and make sense out of what we see in reference to the particular shade of the lenses. If this is so it then becomes extremely important to understand more about this distorted vision.

One might ask first how it is that we come to possess a particular preunderstanding. The general answer given is "from our environment." Alfred North Whitehead draws our attention to the influence of the environment and of science in particular on our preunderstanding:

> The mentality of an epoch springs from the view of the world which is, in fact, dominant in the educated sections of the communities in question. There may be more than one scheme, corresponding to cultural divisions. The various human interests which suggest cosmologies, and also are influenced by them are science, ethics, and religion. In every age each of these topics suggests a view of the world. Insofar as the same set of people are swayed by all, or more than one of these interests, their effective outlook will be the joint production of these sources. But each age has a dominant preoccupation; and during the three centuries in question (the last three), the cosmology derived from science has been asserting itself at the expense of older points of view with their origins elsewhere.[25]

This environmental conditioning, as Whitehead implies, includes a wide range of historical, cultural, social, and psychological factors. We are conditioned by our nationality, our identification with our nation's political and economic developments, its traditions and institutions, and its current place in world affairs. We are influenced by our culture and by the very language we speak. No less important in the formation of our preunderstanding are religious, political, and educational exposures, social and economic status, family relationships, group associations, and our vocational choice. The list could be extended indefinitely. We perceive and interpret reality in a particular way because of this conditioning. This is not to suggest a simple reductionist determinism. It is merely to acknowledge the obvious influence of factors such as these and to suggest that they help shape the preunderstanding out of which we view reality.

In assessing the role of preunderstanding another factor which must be taken into account is the way in which the self interacts with our conditioning. Here it is important to underline the distinction between the terms *self* and *preunderstanding*. The former refers to that which is given in existence itself—that which is common to all human beings, such as intelligence, feeling, consciousness, etc.; the latter refers to that which is a product of the interaction between our environmental conditioning and the self. One way to describe this process is to say that our environment supplies the raw material out of which we frame preunderstanding. Although perhaps an oversimplification it nevertheless remains true that there is an external environment that surrounds us and certain internal givens which react to the environmental stimuli, but it is difficult here in an introductory chapter on hermeneutics to separate the two and clarify their relationship.

Although it is not possible to offer a definitive solution here, though, there is a specific reason to call attention to this interaction—namely, to point out that preunderstanding is a product of this mutuality between the internal and the external. Few would question that our environment feeds and gives form to our mind and emotions. Yet it is equally true that the self shapes and "makes sense" out of the environment. One resulting product of this mutual interaction is preunderstanding. Another reason for calling attention to this process of interaction is to emphasize that we are not simply acted upon by our environment. We may be participants in the formation of our own preunderstanding. We may exercise our intelligence and freedom in the conscious endorsement of assumptions and attitudes with which we approach a given subject. This leads to a final reason for this discussion of the process of interaction: the quality of the self (the level of intelligence, the depth of feeling, etc.) and the richness of the environment and the way in which they mingle will determine the type and functional value of the preunderstandings which we possess.

A Taxonomy of Preunderstanding

In addition to considering the ways in which we come to possess a particular preunderstanding, it will be helpful to consider possible ways of classifying the various types. Preunderstanding is defined as "a body of assumptions and attitudes that a person brings to the perception and interpretation of reality." The pressing question now is: how do we classify the myriad forms in which these assumptions and attitudes appear?

It is possible to discern at least four categories of preunderstanding. Bear in mind that there may be some overlapping between them and that any single act of preunderstanding may and most often does contain elements of all four categories.

The first type of preunderstanding may be described as *informational,* that is the information that one already possesses about any given subject prior to approaching it. This is preunderstanding of the most basic kind, and terms such as *prepossession* and, to a degree, *preconception, prenotion,* and *predetermination* belong here. Seldom, if ever, though, can this category be isolated.

A second type of preunderstanding may be termed *attitudinal.* Though a broad category, essentially what is meant is the disposition that one brings to a given subject. Here such terms as *predisposition, prejudice, bias, life-bearing,* and *life-relation* are appropriate.

A third type of preunderstanding may be called *ideological.* This category would include both a general aspect—the way we view the total complex of reality (*worldview, life-attitude, life-posture, frame of reference, framework,* and *horizon of understanding*)—and a particular aspect—the way we view a specific subject (*point of view, viewpoint, perspective, outlook, onlook,* and *standpoint*). The terms *preconception, prenotion,* and *predetermination* also belong to and may actually fit more comfortably in this category.

The final category is labeled *methodological*—that is, the actual approach which one takes in the explication of a given subject. Terms such as *presupposition, model* and *construct* have meaning in this context. To call a method (e.g., scientific, historical, inductive, etc.) a preunderstanding may appear questionable, but in one sense they do function in the same way as any other type of preunderstanding—they are assumed in an interpretive piece of work and influence the results. Yet in another sense, these methods are tools of neutrality, employed to insure against the effects of certain recognized types of preunderstanding.

The classification of the various types of preunderstanding leads to another important issue: that of categorizing the ways in which a preunderstanding may *function* within an interpretation of reality. The following categories suggest ways that preunderstanding may influence interpretation:

1. Preunderstanding may function as either a *negative* or *positive* influence on interpretation. The negative influence is more readily apparent. It is possible that our preunderstanding may distort our perception of things so that we are really not in touch with reality at all, or only minimally. That our minds are filled with all sorts of ideas, experiences, customs, and aspirations, many of them unconscious, is certain to be the source of much of our trouble. On the positive side, it must also be recognized that preunderstanding is a necessary precondition for understanding reality. Without some frame of reference, in fact, there would be no reality to perceive.

The fact that our minds are not *tabula rasa* makes knowledge possible at all.[26] For example, certain approaches to truth lend themselves to filtering and controlling the possible negative influence of preunderstanding (e.g., a distorting prejudice), while others may require the positive, creative influence of preunderstanding. The scientific method with its controls and checks is designed to produce the maximum degree of objectivity, whereas a work of art will have no value without the artist's creative participation in the subject. It is important to note that some aspects of reality are either so subtle or so constituted that only those observers with a certain kind of preunderstanding are able to perceive and interpret them at all.

2. Preunderstanding may function in either a *comprehensive* or *limited* manner. It may influence the way one views the total sphere of reality or only the way one views fragments of it. For example, if one believes in God, this preunderstanding might, at least theoretically, influence the way one views most, if not all, of reality. This is a preunderstanding which is comprehensive in scope. On the other

hand, if one assumes that all human beings are entitled to equal rights before the law, this preunderstanding will influence one's legal and political views but have nothing to do with the way one studies the stars. This preunderstanding has a more limited application. Implicit in this distinction is the notion that a person may have any number of preunderstandings that apply in different contexts.

3. Preunderstanding may function either *dependently* or *independently* in relation to other preunderstandings that the interpreter possesses. A particular person may for example have one comprehensive preunderstanding that contains within it a number of more limited presuppositions. In this case there will exist some kind of dependent relationship between the comprehensive preunderstanding and the limited presuppositions. On the other hand, between limited presuppositions held in regard to totally different subjects there may exist complete independence.

4. Preunderstanding may function *consistently* or *inconsistently.* It may contain only harmonious elements or it may contain elements that are mutually contradictory. One may, for example, strongly disapprove of policies that exist in South Africa because of a preunderstanding which affirms the equality of all human beings before God. Consistency might seem to require that similar disapproval be displayed in other contexts where racial discrimination exists. Yet this same person may be instrumental in blocking the entrance of a black Christian into church membership. Somewhere within this person's preunderstanding regarding human beings are assumptions or attitudes which operate at cross-purposes. On this matter of consistency it is important to recognize the distinction between what may be logically prior, i.e., factors upon which an argument depends for validity, and what is temporally prior, i.e., what an individual may have assumed in a preunderstanding before one began an interpretive piece of work. An interpretation may be inherently consistent (e.g., a Marxist view of history) but unacceptable because of its starting point (that all history can be understood in terms of class conflict). Consistency does not imply acceptability.

5. Preunderstanding may function *consciously* or *unconsciously.* An individual may interpret reality without knowing that one does so from a particular frame of reference or, on the other hand, be very

aware of the starting point. One may, for instance, consistently prefer Democrats to Republicans, but may or may not be aware of why there is such a preference. The presence of an unconscious element points to another category of classification.

6. Preunderstanding may function as either a *major* or a *minor* influence on an interpretation. It may largely determine the conclusions that an interpreter reaches, or it may only be distantly related to those conclusions. This point becomes evident when a distinction is made between those forms of preunderstanding which necessarily lead to a specific conclusion and those which do not. James Barr makes such a distinction:

> We might distinguish between cases where a particular position will, if presupposed, necessarily lead to a certain result, and cases where the "presupposition" . . . has proved useful in all sorts of relations but which nevertheless has not resulted in uniform results such as might be expected to follow from a logically coercive presupposition.[27]

This latter type of presupposition, of which the historical method serves as a good example, will merely set the broad limits within which a judgment may be reached.

7. Preunderstanding may function *rationally* or *irrationally.* It may be based soundly or the product of some panic reaction. It may be reasonable or the result of a deep-seated neurosis. It may be as rational as the law of noncontradiction or as irrational as a conviction that all college professors are malicious.

8. Finally, preunderstanding may be *open-ended* or *closed*. By virtue of its structure it may allow itself to be corrected and altered by evidence, or conversely, it may reject *a priori* anything which does not nicely fit into some preconceived mold.

If it is true that various types of preunderstanding functioning in a variety of ways are always present in the perception and interpretation of reality, then the question that inevitably arises is whether knowledge of things as they are in themselves is ever possible. From what has been said so far, one might assume that a case was being made for subjectivism—a proposition is true only from the standpoint of a given observer. There has certainly been a historical temptation to engage in the denial of objectivity since each person inevitably sees the world from a particular point of view. But there *is* apparently a real world of objects that have independent existence about which we can gain knowledge. The subjective hypothesis simply does not account for all of reality—what has been traditionally known as the "brute facts" of the world.

There are objects in the external world that give evidence of their own continuity even when they are not observed by human beings. In addition, even though we peer at reality through the shaded glass of our own preunderstanding, this does not mean we do not see reality as it is. It only means that we have to account for the shaded glass in some way—that we *may not see* things as they truly are. The point of hermeneutical studies, then, is not to advocate epistemological subjectivism but to stress that all knowledge is elusive, and to grasp it demands a great deal of effort on our part, not the least of which is keeping a watchful eye on our own personal and societal forms of preunderstanding.

Our particular concern is to see how it is that our preunderstanding is related to gaining knowledge of God as we interpret what we consider to be traces of God's presence and activity in history recorded for us in biblical literature. To do this, it will be helpful to distinguish what have been traditionally called levels of knowledge. These are: (1) knowledge of bodies, (2) knowledge of other minds, (3) knowledge of one's own mind, (4) knowledge of values and universals, and (5) knowledge of God.[28]

In order to gain a knowledge of any level, it is necessary to possess an appropriate preunderstanding that correlates with what is to be interpreted at that level. An appropriate preunderstanding means that generally four factors must be present: (1) there must be a certain amount of correct information about what is to be interpreted; (2) there must be an attitude present that is open and receptive to making contact with the subject to be interpreted; (3) there must be an ideological structure that is sufficiently flexible and adaptable to treat fairly and objectively that which is to be interpreted; and (4) there must be a methodological approach that is appropriate to the subject to be interpreted.

The correlation between the preunderstanding and the subject to be interpreted, however, is not always a simple one-to-one relationship, i.e., one specific preunderstanding for every subject. On the contrary, one comprehensive preunderstanding may be adequate for any number of subjects. The point is rather that certain subjects demand the presence of a particular preunderstanding before full comprehension is possible. Often the understanding of certain aspects of reality eludes those with inappropriate preunderstanding. Some "get nothing out of" Beethoven and others still believe the earth to be flat. Their preunderstanding makes them closed to the meaning of the signals sent in their direction by musical tones and scientific evidence. John McIntyre underscores this general point when he argues for the necessity of an attitude which can adequately deal with the "given" in Christology.[29]

He makes the further point that the given also determines the method which must be employed in analyzing the given. He says: "We are, therefore, in fact now taking a further step and saying that the given not only determines the appropriate attitude to adopt towards it; it also prescribes the method we must follow in its explication."[30] Since our concern is knowledge of God, the task becomes one of finding the preunderstanding appropriate for such knowledge.

Biblical witness suggests that such knowledge comes by *faith*. Faith is *the* preunderstanding which is able to rightly grasp God's self-disclosure. Human faith is the correlative preunderstanding of divine revelation. It is by faith that we are able to perceive and interpret the reality of God.

At this point the question of whether it is legitimate to refer to faith as a preunderstanding arises. It might be argued that faith is rather that which preunderstanding influences. True, one aspect of faith directly apprehends God; faith so conceived is then more of an immediate apprehension of God than a prior understanding about God. While this view may call attention to one important dimension of faith, it does not preclude faith as preunderstanding, for underlying this view are assumptions about God's existence and also attitudes of trust and openness to the divine presence. Such a body of assumptions and attitudes—which makes up a large portion of what faith is—certainly is within the range of the definition of preunderstanding. Thus the conception of faith as an immediate awareness of

God does not exhaust all that the biblical authors and the church have understood as faith. Faith also contains these other dimensions.

Faith, in fact, as used here has at least two dimensions.[31] First, faith contains a cognitive element, i.e., faith *that* God is and has acted in certain ways. The word is used as bare intellectual assent by only one author of the New Testament (James 2:14–26), and then with an ironic twist. The cognitive element is more often regarded as right belief about God (e.g., Jude 3). Such a use of the term implies both informational and ideological assumptions. Although this cognitive element is not the only one, it is certainly foundational. To say that we have knowledge of God we must at least have some correct information and ideas about God. For our purposes, we will say that the minimum cognitive component consists of a belief that God is and was made known in a variety of ways, chief of which for the Christian is Jesus. It is this central belief of Christians, that "God was in Christ," which is assumed in this volume and which becomes then the primary subject of hermeneutical reflection.

A second dimension of the biblical doctrine of faith is the attitude or complex of attitudes called trust, i.e., faith *in* God. We are exhorted to trust God. Such trust becomes efficacious (e.g., Ephesians 2:8, 9). In Pauline terms, we are justified *by* faith. This category of faith involves a personal dimension that carries us beyond the first category of cognition. To know God by trusting is not so much to say that we know about God as it is to say that we know God as a person who relates to us. John Hick describes the nature of faith in the following way.

> Thus the primary religious perception, or basic act of religious interpretation, is not described as either a reasoned conclusion or an unreasoned hunch that there is a God. It is, putatively, an apprehension of the divine presence within the believer's human experience. It is not an inference to a general truth, but a "divine-human encounter," a mediated meeting with the living God.[32]

Thus we may be said to be in a position to gain knowledge of God when we possess a minimum of correct information and ideas about God and are personally related to God. Faith is *the* necessary preunderstanding for a full comprehension of God because it corresponds to the nature of the given. It alone contains the appropriate assumptions and attitudes that make it possible for us to apprehend God.

Earlier in this century, logical positivism, which excludes traditional metaphysics and theology as legitimate forms of knowledge, demonstrated what the solution to the epistemological problem would be if faith played no part in preunderstanding. This philosophical movement argued that only that which is empirically verifiable can be legitimately considered knowledge; some members tried to show by linguistic analysis that other traditional forms of knowledge (e.g., knowledge of God) were impossible. "God-talk" was an emotive expression, not a description of reality. In the last several years, though, there has been a softening of this position. There is now a more general willingness to recognize as acceptable other types of knowledge and language if a good case can be made for them.

Several issues regarding this assertion that faith is *the* preunderstanding necessary for a knowledge of God now surface. The first is this: when faith is defined in this way, is there the implication that the person of faith is somehow freed from any spatio-temporal point of view in coming to an understanding of God? The answer, of course, is no. A believer's faith may be genuine and efficacious, but this does not mean that its contours are not shaped by the environment of which it is a part. The position might best be described by saying that our relationship with God is made secure by faith but that we understand that relationship of faith in terms of the thought-forms of our surroundings. The assumptions and attitudes of faith will always be influenced by temporal concerns and by its place in history; thus it will inevitably be expressed in the categories that are a part of our culture.

Obversely, this further means that if we are to have the clearest possible conception of God, our environment must be such as to continually expose us to God's self-revelation which for the Christian is centered in Jesus Christ. The preunderstanding of faith must be sustained in a community (the church) which is both continuous with the historical act of revelation and through which God's own self-revelation continues. It means also that if our conception of God is to be accurate, we need constantly to test and refine the content of our faith by placing it over and against the biblical documents which attest to historical revelation. Only in this way can we keep our faith close to its necessary source of sustenance—the Bible.

A third matter involves the way in which faith functions in preunderstanding. Though this point will be expanded later, it will serve us well to make two initial observations: (1) though faith is a gift of God, it is still a human possession. It may, for example, contain inconsistent and irrational elements and function as a negative influence on interpretation. In other words, there is really no such thing as "pure" faith, and thus the preunderstanding of faith may be functionally described in the same manner as any other preunderstanding; (2) because faith is formed out of a specific culture and expressed in terms of it, our understanding of God and interpretations of the historical and biblical material attesting to this revelation in Jesus Christ will tend to reflect this culture.[33] It follows that the preunderstanding of faith may serve merely to set the broad limits within which a wide range of interpretations may be reached depending on the interpreter's total life environment.

Though faith contains the minimum necessary informational, attitudinal, and ideological factors for a knowledge of God, this fact is only sufficient to guarantee that an adequate method of explication of that knowledge is available. As implied already, for the Christian the knowledge of God which is sought comes by God's self-disclosure in Jesus Christ. The lot is clearly cast on the side of revelation rather than natural theology. If knowledge of God comes via Jesus Christ, the method of explication necessarily involves us in doing history. As John Hick says: "In Christianity, the catalyst of faith is the person of Jesus Christ. It is in the historical figure of Jesus the Christ that, according to the Christian claim, God has in a unique and final way disclosed Himself to man."[34] To give a full account of our knowledge of God as revealed in Jesus Christ it will be necessary to employ the critical tools of historical study as part of an adequate preunderstanding for the interpretation of the Christian faith.

There is one final matter that has remained implicit but now needs to be made explicit, namely, the precise relationship between knowledge, preunderstanding, and interpretation. The knowledge that is being sought is the knowledge of God. Further, one may be said to gain such knowledge only when one possesses the preunderstanding of faith. But the preunderstanding of faith is dependent upon God's historical self-disclosure in Jesus Christ attested to in Scripture. The relationship of these elements might be clarified by saying that we endeavor to gain knowledge of God by interpreting the historical and biblical data surrounding the Christ-Event from within the preunderstanding of faith. It must be admitted that there is a circularity involved in this relationship, i.e., that the preunderstanding of faith in interpretation presupposes some knowledge of God. Yet all interpretation proceeds on the condition that the interpreter has some prior understanding, however limited, of that which is to be interpreted. There is a reciprocal relationship between our preunderstanding and the matter to be interpreted. The preunderstanding that we already possess gives us the capacity to penetrate the work to be interpreted. As we do so, the content of what we are interpreting acts upon our preünderstanding to enlarge it, modify it, or change it as the case may be.

Several issues have been raised along the way in this preliminary discussion of hermeneutics. As the attempt is made to clarify the issues of biblical interpretation, the one needing further attention at this point is the way in which the interpreter of Scripture brings assumptions about the Bible to the interpretive task.

SUGGESTED READING

Barr, James. *Old and New in Interpretation*. New York: Harper and Row, 1966.

Bultmann, Rudolf. "The Problem of Hermeneutics." In *Essays*. New York: Macmillan, 1955.

Evans, Donald D. *The Logic of Self-Involvement*. London: SCM, 1963.

Hick, John. *Faith and Knowledge*. Ithaca, New York: Cornell University, 1959.

Macquarrie, John. *God-Talk*. New York: Harper and Row, 1967.

Merleau-Ponty, Maurice. *The Phenomenology of Perception*. London: Routledge and Kegan Paul, 1962.

Polanyi, Michael. *The Tacit Dimension*. London: Routledge and Kegan Paul, 1967.

2

Hermeneutics: The Critical Assumptions

The Presence of Assumptions

To assert that faith and historical method are basic to any attempt to adequately interpret the Christian faith is not a position with which everyone would agree. Neither is there any guarantee, even among those who would agree and approach the Scriptures with these assumptions, that there will be a unity of interpretive results. The preunderstanding of the interpreter, even when it includes a faith posture and a rigorous historical approach, generally incorporates a wide variety of other assumptions as well. These other assumptions will influence the outcome of the hermeneutical effort. Across the history of the church these assumptions have generally revolved around the nature of the Bible and more particularly the intersecting concepts of revelation, the Word of God, inspiration, authority, tradition, and function. This chapter is an attempt to define and categorize these assumptions about the Bible and in so doing to suggest some places to begin the crucial task of interpreting the Scriptures.[1]

The Nature of the Bible

ITS UNITY

Classical textbooks on hermeneutics often speak about, or occasionally merely assume, the unity of the Bible. Terry remarks that "it is of the first importance to observe that, from a Christian point of view, the Old Testament cannot be fully apprehended without the help of the New,"[2] implying an interconnectedness of the Testaments. But given the more obvious diversity contained in the Bible, especially between the two Testaments, one might well ask whether the unity is more in the mind of the theologian than in the Bible. That is, is the unity which the interpreter "finds" really inherent in the data of the Scriptures, or is it imposed by the theologian's ideological system? Invariably the interpreter attempts to make unified sense out of the diverse elements. But even granting this tendency and fully acknowledging the diversity of Scripture, it is still possible to speak about an essential unity. Several categories have been used by theologians and biblical scholars in the attempt to express the unity which is apparently inherent to the Bible.

Karl Barth, not unlike his precritical predecessors, assumes the unity of the Bible and the inseparability of the Testaments. For him Jesus Christ is the revelatory center of the New Testament, and indeed all Scripture including the Old Testament focuses in Christ. In Christ is the fullness of God's self-revelation come, and all of Scripture points to this primary self-disclosure. Thus, for example, the meaning of the creation account cannot be fully understood from reading the Genesis account but only after there is a theological integration of creator and creation in the personhood of Jesus Christ.[3]

In proposing a revised form of typological exegesis, Gerhard von Rad develops a related argument. He maintains that the warrant for his proposal is found in the tradition-building process which continually projects the future hope in the form of analogies of the past. The New Testament, he argues, should be viewed as the final result of Israel's interpretation of her tradition, the Christ-event being the climax of divine intervention in Israel's future-oriented history.[4]

Another "theological" solution to the problem of unity is the structure of promise and fulfillment which is deeply rooted in the Bible itself. The basic premise of this view is that God has a grand design for the faithful which embraces the events of history. Israel understood the purpose of God in terms of a promise for the future, and the New Testament community understood the Christ-event as the fulfillment of the promise. A similar view is found in the idea of the covenant which provides the unifying center to the Bible.[5]

A third view more popular in a previous generation is progressive revelation. This position maintains that God gradually unfolded the divine will and purpose for humankind over the centuries. Primitive animistic and nomadic religions came early and rested at the bottom of the scale, while the religion of Jesus represented the apex of religious development. A reassessment of the religious views of the prophetic period in the Old Testament has made this view less persuasive. In the Mosaic period, for example, there are both primitive and advanced prophetic forms of religion existing alongside of each other. The simple evolutionary scheme which undergirded the notion of progressive revelation does not entirely match with the evidence of history.

H. H. Rowley, in his book *The Unity of the Bible,* prefers to find unity in the common themes which recur in the writings of the different authors of Scripture. The presence of concepts about God, human nature, sin, and election are present in both Testaments. Yet, the presence of similar concepts in both Testaments does not provide an adequate basis for unity unless that unity can be demonstrated to be organic. Otherwise it would be possible to argue for a unity between the Bible and many other religious books such as the Koran, which is a different sort of unity than implied in Rowley's thesis.

A final concept, which has been used by the church for centuries in preserving the unity of Scripture, is canon. Canon comes from a semitic word meaning "reed" and was expanded to denote a measuring reed or rod used in construction. Figuratively, the word came to mean the regulating norm, and in the case of the church the authoritative sacred books composing the Old and New Testaments. These sixty-six books (excluding the Apocrypha) became the Scripture of the church and were viewed as the rule of faith and conduct. The Old Testament canon was agreed upon only after hundreds of years of pondering and debate. Some books were eliminated because they were judged to be spiritually inferior or did not appear to be authentic statements of what God was trying to communicate to the faithful. The New Testament canon was also slow in developing; it did not reach its present form until the fourth century. The value of the concept of canonicity is that it affirms the unity of Scripture on the basis of the testimony of a multitude of witnesses scattered over several centuries. These witnesses, divided by language and culture, speak a common word about the one God who had the same redemptive purpose for humanity and who was alive and real for each of them.

The traditional view of the canon, which assumes an unbroken continuity between the writing and the collecting of an authoritative body of Scripture, is not possible to hold, however, in light of a historical understanding of what actually took place. Even the reconstruction of the historical development involved in the formation of canon is not easily done, though the fact that there was such a history is incontrovertible. The value of the concept of canon as a way of preserving the unity of Scripture for the church resides then not in ignoring history but in affirming the historical nature of the biblical witness. There is no "revelation" apart from the experience of the history of Israel and the coming of Jesus. The formation of the literature which registers this experience is a part of Israel's history, and it witnesses to the way in which God entered into the experience and history of the human family.[6]

Each of these attempts to find an essential unity in the Bible has its respective weakness, but taken together they point to a unity that is not simply imposed by an interpreter onto the Bible. The Bible is a collection of writings from authors who across the centuries have been united in their testimony to the redeeming love of God. For it is undeniably the activity of God with humankind recorded in the Bible that gives the Bible its essential unity.

ITS DIVERSITY

To speak of the Bible's unity in no way minimizes its diversity. The diversity of the Scriptures is apparent to all who attempt to read them. Several differences come immediately to mind:

1. *Distinctions Between the Old Testament and the New Testament:* The Old Testament is the story of a people and a nation—their beliefs, history, leaders, worship, customs, and literature. The New Testament is the account of Jesus and the community that formed around him. There are many connecting links but two separate stories. Concepts such as promise and fulfillment or unified witness to God's gracious activity do not overcome the obvious differences between the Testaments.

2. *Different Languages:* The primary language of the Old Testa-

ment is Hebrew. The New Testament is written in Greek, based in part on some Aramaic sources which are now lost. The particular Greek used, called *koinē,* was the common idiom of the entire Mediterranean world during the New Testament era. These different languages, which express the thoughts and culture of different peoples, serve to underline the distinction between the Testaments.

3. *Different Eras and Cultures:* The composition of the Bible took more than 1,300 years. The Old Testament developed from about 1200 B.C. to 100 B.C.; the New Testament was essentially written in the first century A.D. All of the Old Testament authors were Jews as were those of the New Testament with the exception of Luke. The writing of the Old Testament took place in Palestine, Babylonia, and surrounding areas. With one or two exceptions it is difficult to say precisely where the New Testament books were written, although all of the books were most certainly penned in the lands surrounding the Mediterranean.

4. *Different Types of Literature:*

In the Old Testament:

Legal: Genesis, Exodus, Leviticus, Numbers, Deuteronomy (5 total).

Historical: Joshua, Judges, Ruth, 1 and 2 Samuel, 1 and 2 Kings, 1 and 2 Chronicles, Ezra, Nehemiah, Esther (12 total).

Poetical: Job, Psalms, Proverbs, Ecclesiastes, Song of Solomon (5 total).

Prophetic: (a) Major Prophets: Isaiah, Jeremiah, Lamentations, Ezekiel, Daniel (5 total).
(b) Minor Prophets: Hosea, Joel, Amos, Obadiah, Jonah, Micah, Nahum, Habakkuk, Zephaniah, Haggai, Zechariah, Malachi (12 total).

In the New Testament:

Historical: The Gospels: Matthew, Mark, Luke, John, Acts (5 total).

Doctrinal: The Epistles: Romans, 1 and 2 Corinthians, Galatians, Ephesians, Philippians, Colossians, 1 and 2 Thessalonians, 1 and 2 Timothy, Titus, Philemon, Hebrews, James, 1 and 2 Peter, 1, 2, and 3 John, Jude (21 total).

Apocalyptic: Revelation (1 total).

There is some risk in dividing the biblical literature into these traditional canonical categories. The insights of modern historical scholarship suggest that this division has limitations, and may in fact be misleading. Daniel, for example, might be better classified as apocalyptic, and certainly many of the books of the Bible contain elements of diverse types of literature. But the list is presented here for reference and to underline the point that there are many genres in the Bible. Each of these forms of literature has its own distinctive features and requirements for fair and accurate interpretation, and thus an attempt will be made below to give some hermeneutical guidelines for each genre.

5. *Distinctions Between the Various Books of the Bible:* The various authors of the books of the Bible give to their writing their own personal stamp. They have their own idiosyncrasies, natural talents, and levels of knowledge. They develop their thoughts in reference to their life situation and culture. They speak to the differing situations and needs of the people to whom they are addressing the literature. Thus the literature that edifies, nurtures, and gives hope to captives in Babylon will be quite different from that which clarifies family relations in Corinth in the first century. Such differences arise not only between the Testaments but also within each Testament as well. For example, very early in the development of biblical criticism, scholars pointed to the difference between the Gospels and the writings of Paul. More recent scholarship has stressed the sharp redactional differences within the New Testament corpus. Such biblical scholars, in an effort to make "hermeneutical sense" out of the differences in the New Testament, have argued for a canon within the canon, often giving a central place to the thought of Paul.[7]

ITS CHARACTER AND STYLE

It is not easy to describe the character and style of the Bible as though there were one author from a single culture using one language. Some generalizations, however, still may be useful as a guide for the interpretation of Scripture:

1. The Reformers, in reaction to the Catholic Church's reluctance to allow laypeople access to the Bible, postulated the perspicuity of

Scripture. Given the internal witness of the Spirit, what is necessary to know for salvation is clearly expressed in Scripture and may be easily understood by all. They believed that the Bible was sufficiently clear for all Christians to read it, and it was reprehensible to them that any Christians should be forbidden from doing so. It is not difficult to agree with the Reformers' point, but one should be careful not to take the next step—to say that the Bible is a simple book, direct and clear in all it says. The Bible is a very *complex book*. The concepts are subtle, and the writing is occasionally obscure, hidden behind centuries of history and the barriers of language and culture. Some parts are direct and simple; these can easily be understood by any literate person who has some acquaintance with the biblical world. Other parts remain out of reach for the average reader or anyone who does not have a grasp of the history and culture of biblical times and a training in critical methodology. Thus to assert that the Bible as a whole is clear and simple is to go against the experience most of us have as we read it. To be fair, though, the Reformers were making a different point related to understanding God's gracious love.

2. The Bible, again with a few obvious exceptions (e.g., genealogies and lists), has a *liveliness and beauty of style* almost unparalleled. There are parts of the Bible that do not immediately impress the reader as elegant, eloquent, and cogent, but taken as a whole the Bible is an impressive body of literature. The language, especially in the Old Testament, is often vivid and concrete. Illustrations are frequently drawn from the world of nature. There is extensive use of figurative and picturesque language. Metaphor and symbol are commonly used and have a way of capturing the attention of the reader. The New Testament, as the story of Jesus, has its own poignancy apart from any religious purpose.

3. Another generalization about the Bible involves its great *diversity of style*. Nearly every use of language with which we are familiar occurs some place in the Bible. A wide variety of human experiences have been recorded and a multitude of ways of communicating the meaning of those experiences have been utilized. Without a sensitive understanding of the many ways language is used, the Bible will forever remain an elusive book.

4. The biblical authors are often *anthropomorphic and anagogical*—and necessarily so, especially in speaking about certain themes such as the primary subject of God. They speak of God's attributes and actions through the use of images, symbols, allegories, similes, and metaphors. There are few so-called propositional statements about God in Scripture; more often the deity is described by reference to an event or custom common in the culture. For example, God's almightiness is spoken of in terms of a right arm because the right arm was viewed as the stronger of the two, and with it the most powerful blows were delivered. Thus to fully understand the Bible's "storyline," the reader must appreciate the lyric character of the biblical language.

5. Finally, the Bible deals with the *most important and pressing questions of human existence*. Who is God and how is God's self-disclosure manifest? How does the human family relate to God? What is the nature of human nature? What are the dimensions of the human experience? How do we deal with suffering and death? How should we live our lives? These are the questions to which the Bible speaks and for which a desperate world longs for answers.

Concepts About the Bible

There are a number of concepts commonly used in discussing the nature of the Bible. As the interpreter begins the task of drawing from the Bible material for "doing" theology, preparing a sermon, giving comfort and guidance, or making ethical judgments, these concepts come into play and influence the interpretive results. It is therefore of vital importance to be clear about the many shades of meaning of these terms.[8]

REVELATION

Revelation has been understood by the church across the centuries as the process which God uses to become known to human beings. Christianity, often described as a "revealed religion," has consistently held that humankind could not know God apart from the divine act of self-disclosure. God is not so much discovered by human search as known through the deity's own initiative and self-revelation.

The purpose of God's self-revelation is to manifest love to humankind and to confront them with the divine purpose for their lives in the world. God's self-disclosure presupposes on the part of humankind a capacity for responding to this love and purpose, a response of faith which is a whole-souled commitment to the personhood and will of God.

Biblical revelation is generally acknowledged as historical in nature. To be sure, there is what has been traditionally called *general revelation*. The Apostle Paul writes: "Ever since the creation of the world his invisible nature, namely, his eternal power and deity, has been clearly perceived in the things that have been made" (Romans 1:20). *Special revelation,* though, is necessary for us to know God in a saving way. God is described in the Bible as self-revealing in history through divine actions on behalf of those people chosen of God—and, most decisively of all, in Jesus Christ. Thus the idea of revelation in the Bible is not only historical but personal also. It is not a series of propositions or a mere list of historical facts but a means of confrontation and communication. Even when revelation is reduced to a statement or event as it is in the Scriptures, it is closely tied to God's will and purpose and demands an appropriate response.

Scripture has been understood as the record of God's self-disclosure and of the responses by the people of God to that self-disclosure. Within the theological traditions of the church there has been some difference of opinion on how revelation and the Bible are related. The views are diverse, each has its own subtlety and nuance, but for our purpose these views may be summarized into two broad categories. One view, held firmly by the conservative tradition of the larger church, is to the effect that the Scriptures themselves have become a part of the revelation. The basic assumption behind this point of view is that God inspired the writing of the Bible in such a way as to make it free from error. It constantly is in a state of becoming the divine Word spoken to the people of God. An able spokesman for this position in the Protestant Reformed tradition was the Princeton theologian B. B. Warfield, whose book *Revelation and*

Inspiration is still referred to as the classical statement of the view. He writes:

> It will suffice to remind ourselves that it looks upon the Bible as an oracular book,—as the Word of God in such a sense that whatever it says, God says,—not a book, then, in which one may, by searching, find some word of God, but a book which may be frankly appealed to any point with the assurance that whatever it may be found to say, that is the Word of God.[9]

The second view asserts that the Bible is witness to and testimony of God's revelation. As the divine presence has been made known, individuals have recorded these self-disclosures. The Bible, then, becomes a record of human observation and experience of God's revelation rather than a part of the revelation itself. In this view (or set of views) the critical question about the record becomes its trustworthiness and the way in which God's Word is heard through it.

WORD OF GOD

What is revealed by God is the divine Word. The letter to the Hebrews opens with the declaration that in many ways and at various times God did speak through various prophets and finally through the Son. The content of revelation in this case is the Word of God, a notion that has several shades of meaning in current theological discussion. One commonly held view is that the Word of God and Scripture are essentially synonymous. The Word of God is the Bible—the Old and New Testaments—and they are the inspired rule of faith and practice for Christians. The Bible is the Word of God written.

Another perspective holds that the Word of God refers to the saving activity of God, and in particular the gospel, the message of Jesus Christ as we know it in the New Testament. But in a wider sense the Word of God is the gracious activity of God throughout history, a history that is recorded for us in the whole of the Bible. Faithful believers, led by the Spirit of God but also conditioned by the language and thought forms of the times and cultures in which they lived, gave written witness to God's saving activity. We have in Scripture all that is necessary for our salvation, though this does not mean that the Bible should be used in deciding questions of natural science or in determining the pattern of prehistoric times. But because God speaks to us through the Scriptures, they rightfully may be called the Word of God.

A slightly different view holds that Jesus Christ is the supreme revelation of God, the Word of God in the highest sense—the living Word. The Bible is the essential witness to Jesus Christ, but it does not itself constitute the revelation. God does not reveal books, chapters, and sentences, but rather, the divine self. Although merely a human witness, the Bible is nonetheless a necessary witness in that it provides access to the primary act of revelation in Jesus Christ. Thus the Word of God is not identical with the Bible, but the Bible is essential as the appropriate access to the Word of God.

Another use of the term involves its relation to proclamation. Whenever and wherever the Scriptures and their essential message of God's saving love in Jesus Christ are preached and attentively read under the guidance of the Holy Spirit, there the Word of God is heard.

INSPIRATION

The doctrine of the inspiration of Scripture has generally been utilized as a means of establishing the trustworthiness of the Bible as an authentic record of God's revelation. The Greek term for *inspired,* meaning literally "God-breathed," occurs in 2 Timothy 3:16 in reference to Old Testament Scripture: "All scripture is inspired by God and profitable for teaching, for reproof, for correction, and for training in righteousness." The implication of this passage and other often-quoted ones (2 Peter 1:19–21, John 10:34–38, et al.) is that the Spirit of God infused Scripture with life-giving power and superintended the authors in such a way as to control the content of their writing. The notion of inspiration was familiar in the Greek world as discovered in its oracles, for instance, which were thought of as inspired because they were uttered by people who were believed to be filled by a divine power and controlled by it. The author of 2 Timothy is apparently thinking of the Scriptures as the writings of those under the control and guidance of the divine Spirit.

In just what way the Holy Spirit inspired the authors of Scripture has been hotly debated throughout church history; it continues so today.[10] Again, the conservative wing of the church has maintained what is often called a "high" view of Scripture—a view that understands the Bible to be God's written Word to humankind. Other qualifying adjectives and descriptive phrases generally go along with this position. One conservative theologian lists thirteen characteristics which serve as a good summary:

1. All Scripture is God-breathed,
2. and is God's written word to man,
3. infallible and
4. inerrant,
5. as originally given.
6. Divine inspiration is plenary,
7. verbal, and
8. confluent.
9. As the very Word of God, Scripture possesses the properties of authority,
10. sufficiency,
11. clarity, and
12. efficacy.
13. The central purpose of Scripture is to present Christ.[11]

The rise of historical criticism has made this view somewhat difficult to maintain, and thus several modified views have emerged. One author, for example, has attempted to make a case for the infallibility of Scripture in matters of faith and practice without holding that the Scriptures are inerrant.[12] Others, unwilling to actually admit the possibility of error in Scripture, have developed a view that has been termed limited inerrancy. This position holds that the Bible is inerrant in terms of the intention of the author. The Bible's intention is not to teach us science, but to make us "wise unto salvation." The Bible lives up to this intent and is therefore inerrant.[13]

The general drift of theological thought in our century on the nature of Scripture has been away from concepts such as infallibility and inerrancy. It would take us too far afield to review the entire story, but at least two more broad categories containing a number of carefully constructed positions should be mentioned.

Karl Barth is perhaps the best known theologian representing the view that the Bible is not the inerrantly inspired Word of God. For him Scripture becomes the Word of God as it witnesses to the primary Word, Jesus Christ. Reacting both to scholastic rationalism which viewed Scripture as inerrant and to the more liberal and critical views which were actually more adept at deconstruction than reconstruction, Barth attempts to find a position mediating between the two. Acknowledging the vulnerability of the Bible and its capacity for error, he postulates that the Bible becomes the Word of God as it is proclaimed and used by the Holy Spirit to bear witness to Jesus Christ.[14] One way in which Barth expresses his view is to classify the Word of God into three categories. The primary form is Jesus Christ, the living Word; the secondary form is the Bible, the written Word; and the third is the church's proclamation, the proclaimed Word. In this structure the Bible is not the inspired Word of God but may be said to be inspired as it is a witness to Jesus Christ and is received in faith.

Other biblical scholars less concerned about preserving the trustworthiness and authority of Scripture in the church have addressed the Bible with all the tools of the historical-critical approach. The Bible, inspired as other great works of literature have been inspired, deserves no special status to protect it.

At the risk of oversimplification, let me suggest three categories as a way of summarizing what has been said about the inspiration of Scripture. (1) The Bible *is* the inspired Word of God, an essential part of God's self-disclosure. (2) The Bible *becomes* the Word of God and may be said to be inspired as it is faithfully proclaimed in the church and accepted by faith. (3) The Bible is inspired *only insofar as all great literature is inspired* and should be treated as any other book.

AUTHORITY

Another concept which is widely used in discussions of the status of the Bible is "authority." If God did reveal the divine presence in particular places, times, and events, and if the Scriptures are viewed as a part of this revelation or witness to it, then the Scriptures in themselves begin to take on some of the authority of God. If the Scriptures are the Word of God or become so as God uses them in proclamation, then they carry the "weight" we grant to God.

Authority is a relational or hierarchical term related to power and assigning degrees of influence over us.[15] The term has some similarity to the word "norm" in the sense of controlling, and the Bible may be spoken of as normative, by which is meant it is the final court of appeal. As such, authority defines our relationship to the Bible and the relationship of the Bible to other documents, customs, and traditions.

The amount of authority which the Bible is given hinges on whether it is viewed as truthful or commended to us as truth by another trusted and comparable authority. If it is commended to us as truth as, for example, by the church, then it has a secondary kind of authority. J. K. S. Reid, in arguing for the essential truthfulness of the Bible, suggests that it is fully authoritative because it has the following characteristics: (1) permanent and not dispensable; (2) simple and not esoteric; (3) universal and not merely particular; (4) categorical, allowing no evasion; and (5) commanding assent.[16] In putting forth this view Reid is careful to point out that biblical authority does not rest in immediate applicability but in the intrinsic quality of the whole.

The risk of considering the authority of Scripture as an intrinsic quality is that it raises the same problems associated with inspiration, inerrancy, and infallibility. Yet its subject matter does give credence to the argument from "intrinsic quality" in that it is a book about Jesus Christ and the only book of its kind. It is our primary reference to the pivotal act of God's self-disclosure.[17]

To assert that the Bible's authority derives from a claim by another comparable authority (e.g., the church) is not particularly convincing in the age of "the twilight of authority." Perhaps the strongest case for this external view is made when the Bible is viewed as the means by which God addresses humankind, the place in which the deity confronts them with the divine Word. The Bible then is granted an external authority, the authority of God, who chooses to speak in and through it concerning the events of salvation.

TRADITION

A fifth concept which is central to the interpreter's work is tradition. As the text is approached for sermon or theological reflection, the interpreter does so in the context of a cultural/theological/ecclesiastical tradition. As much as one may think it is possible to be free from such a context, one really cannot escape its influence, nor is it necessarily helpful to do so. Proclamation and theological reflection occur and are meaningful within the thought forms and customs of a culture. Even Luther, in his courageous stand against a binding tradition in his assertion of *sola scriptura,* recovered another tradition which had roots going back to Augustine and Paul.

Tradition is the foundation of a culture, that which holds past and present together. It connects the individual with a larger community and gives categories of understanding and insight for living. What a person knows, believes, and deems important has to a large extent been handed down by word and example. In the religious realm, beliefs, rites, formulations of prayers and hymns, etc. are transmitted with special care.

In the Old Testament there is a tradition which is preserved by Israel and passed on to succeeding generations. This "sacred deposit" embraces all aspects of life and gives Israel its distinctive features, maintaining its continuity over the centuries. There is the deep belief that this tradition is more than a custom but is of divine origin and constitutes the essence of God's will for the nation. It consists of several fixed elements: beliefs, law, and forms of worship. It also develops and progresses with time, however, as God continues to lead the faithful in relation to the specific needs of their situation. In time the tradition takes a written form, although a living tradition continues parallel to the writing.

Tradition plays an important role in the New Testament as well. Jesus serves notice of his independence from the Jewish tradition of his time, although he is loyal to the legacy preserved in Scripture: "Think not that I have come to abolish the law and the prophets; I have come not to abolish them but to fulfill them" (Matt. 5:17). Still, the "tradition of the elders" does not have his full support and he freely speaks of its inadequacy. A new tradition grows up around the teaching of Jesus, a tradition that is preserved in oral teachings and ultimately takes a written form. Gradually, as the early church struggled with all of the problems inherent in the culture of the time, a tradition sprang up around the New Testament documents. The rest is a long and interesting history of councils, confessions, decrees, debates, and schisms. As one approaches the biblical text, it is inevitable that one will do so carrying the assumptions of a given tradition. To be aware of these assumptions and allow them to find their most positive and constructive expression is the sacred responsibility of the interpreter.

FUNCTION

A final category related to the assumptions of the interpreter has to do with the particular functions that Scripture serves in a given context. Function is directly tied to the other critical assumptions to which reference has already been made. This function will vary depending upon the interpreter's views about revelation, Word of God, inspiration, and authority. It will also serve a particular function assigned to it in the interpreter's theological/ecclesiastical tradition. For example, the Bible will function differently in a Catholic or Protestant setting and play a different role in a conservative or liberal setting.

Furthermore, the function which the Bible serves will differ depending upon the purpose of the interpreter. The Bible is used divergently by the exegete, the theologian, the preacher, the moral philosopher, and the spiritual counselor. Although one may desire to work "in accord with Scripture," one may use the Bible variously, depending upon the particular objective. Traditionally, the church has used Scripture for several specific purposes: (1) for theological guidance; (2) for worship; (3) for personal and social ethics; (4) for preaching; and (5) for devotion and spiritual nurture. Each of these uses of Scripture has assumptions guiding its practice, and the outcome of the interpretive effort will vary significantly to fit this purpose.

There are a multitude of causes which people support and for which they find encouragement in Scripture. Scripture is often made to function as a way of giving sanction to the cause. Marxist, feminist, and psychoanalytic readings of Scripture are all possible.[18] The history of interpretation is replete with causes that have been given additional support by a particular handling of Scripture.

Whatever the purpose, interpreting the Bible is not an easy assignment, especially if one is committed to a fair and accurate handling of the text. It involves a basic understanding of the nature of the Bible. It involves an awareness of one's own assumptions about the Bible as revelation, the Bible as the Word of God, the meaning of inspiration, the consequent authority of the Bible, and the tradition out of which one's perspective has been shaped. It also requires that the interpreter be clear regarding the purpose of the interpretive effort and of the Bible's function in fulfilling that purpose. The next step in the interpretation of Scripture is to clarify the relationship between three crucial issues that have been introduced. These issues, revelation, history, and faith, intersect in the Word of God—that is, in Jesus Christ.

SUGGESTED READING

Abraham, William J. *The Divine Inspiration of Scripture*. Oxford: Oxford University, 1981.

Barr, James. *The Bible in the Modern World*. New York: Harper and Row, 1973.

———. *Holy Scripture: Canon, Authority, Criticism*. Philadelphia: Westminster, 1983.

Barth, Karl. *Church Dogmatics*, I/1, I/2. Edinburgh: T. and T. Clark, 1936.

Childs, Brevard S. *Biblical Theology in Crisis*. Philadelphia: Westminster, 1970.

———. *Introduction to the Old Testament as Scripture*. Philadelphia: Fortress, 1979.

Reid, J. K. S. *The Authority of Scripture*. New York: Harper and Brothers, 1957.

Rogers, Jack B., and Donald K. McKim. *The Authority and Interpretation of the Bible: An Historical Approach*. New York: Harper and Row, 1979.

Warfield, B. B. *Revelation and Inspiration*. Oxford: Oxford University, 1927.

3

Hermeneutics: The Crucial Issues

Biblical Faith and History

Although other religious traditions have sought knowledge of God in mystical or rational experience or in nature, the biblical faith has found revelation centered primarily in certain historical events, chief of which is the coming of Christ. This understanding of revelation has involved the Christian theologian in the complex task of defining and interpreting history.

This claim that revelation is in some sense tied to history has not been easy to maintain. In fact, in adjustment to biblical criticism of the last two centuries much of Protestant theology has attempted to shift the ground of revelation from objective historical footing to subjective experience. Some theologians have suggested that the facts of biblical history do not matter so much for the life of faith as does our subjective understanding of Jesus. It has been argued that anthropology, not history, should be the primary concern of Christian thinkers. This argument certainly contains a part of the truth, for there is more to the biblical faith than mere historical fact. A purely historical approach cannot prove that an event has value for the life of faith, and it is certainly true that relationship with God is essentially subjective and personal. But to divorce such subjective experience from its objective basis is to deny the heart of the biblical witness. If no reliance can be placed at any point on biblical accounts of alleged historical events, it becomes hard to see how the specific affirmations made about the work and person of Jesus can be justified.[1] It will be our contention here that the Jesus who actually lived in Palestine is at the center of God's revelatory activity—that he gives faith its base of objectivity and supplies its content.

Hence one of our purposes in this chapter will be to show how any view of revelation which places Jesus at the center of God's self-disclosure must take his history and consequently historical interpretation seriously. A further purpose is to connect faith and history in an effort to discern how it is possible for us truly to hear the Word of God. Revelation, history, and faith are the crucial issues of hermeneutics.

Revelation and History in Modern Theology

Traditional Roman Catholicism and Protestant Orthodoxy have broken very little from the historic conception of Scripture as the unified web of revealed truth. Both root revelation in the historical appearance of Jesus, yet their positions tend to avoid the real complexities of the historical interpretation by stressing the supposed infallibility of interpretation by each respective inspired prophet or Apostle. Both see the Bible as the written Word of God, asserting that it contains clear-cut propositions about the Christ-event and other doctrinal matters which can be rationally discerned. Hence the answers to what happened in the history surrounding the revelatory events are predisposed. Historical investigation may fill in the background but not change the conclusions. Although miles apart on other issues, these two groups do share this positing of propositional revelation as contained in Scripture.

For the traditional Catholic, what is not revealed by the light of nature or rational knowledge comes from God by direct "communication, delivered for our belief."[2] It is maintained intact by the tradition of the church. Though it is true that some modern Catholic theologians have given more emphasis to historical "event" as a mode of revelation, they still fall back on "revealed dogma" as the primary focus of our knowledge of God.[3]

Even in the harsh winds of biblical criticism, Protestant Orthodoxy continues to identify the words of Scripture with God's revealing Word.[4] Indeed, the more conservative wing of the church continues to limit the ground of religious authority *to* the Bible. The Bible, and the Bible only, is for them the written Word of God, and this written Word is the propositional revelation of Christ's will. It is only propositional revelation that can clarify the state of the sinner before a holy God.

Many conservative theologians are careful to point out that Jesus Christ is the central revelation of God and that to conceive of the Bible as the primary revelation is heresy; yet by postulating biblical inerrancy the real problem of historical interpretation is evaded. Thus both traditional Roman Catholicism and Protestant Orthodoxy, while anchoring revelation firmly to history, have nevertheless found it possible to stay on the edges of the difficult question of the interpretation of history by equating revelation with Scripture or with Scripture and tradition.

This sort of conclusion, though, hardly solves the problem. Historical questions cannot be so easily pushed aside.[5] In fact, since the rise of biblical criticism few Christians have been able to make so easy an identification of God's Word with the written words of Scripture. In Protestant theology of the nineteenth and twentieth centuries, there has been a continuous search for a category of experience that would get to the root of revelation buried beneath the layers of tradition documented in Scripture. The Protestant theologian has often asked the question of revelation in a much more radical way than the Catholic who, in Vatican II, continued to debate over the sources of revelation—whether it is totally contained in Scripture or includes tradition also. The Protestant, however, asks with great intensity: where can revelation be found *at all,* if it cannot be equated with Scripture? For both the Catholic and the Protestant, though, revelation remains a crucial issue.

In addition to the rise of historical criticism, Kant's rejection of natural theology and emphasis on epistemology have made the concept of revelation important to the theological discussion. Many modern theologies have thus had first to establish themselves as theologies of revelation, assuming that the concept of revelation is the most comprehensive expression of the uniqueness of the Christian faith.[6] It is interesting to note that the term *revelation* has acquired this centrality and importance only within the last century; the church, up until that time, found other categories in which to express its faith.[7] Some have argued that the concept of revelation has been given far more significance than it merits; they believe that other categories (e.g., reconciliation, Christian existence, etc.) are better suited to describe the essence of the Christian faith.[8] One author has specifically questioned whether Christianity has a revelation at all, and others on the "frontline" of theological change have preferred to theologize in other frameworks.[9] Yet on the whole, it has been difficult for modern theology not to begin with the inquiry: how do you know? as a result of the increased emphasis on epistemological concerns in dealing either with statements of revelation or with the question of the uniqueness of Jesus as the revealer of God.

The concept of revelation at the center of modern theology reflects the historical and epistemological sensitivity of our times. In contrast to the theologians of the Middle Ages and the Enlightenment, who saw revelation either in reason or in direct communication from God, the modern theologian invariably links revelation to history in some manner. Prior to the nineteenth century, there was "no appreciation of a revelation mediated through successive situations in a real history."[10] But the modern theologian, it appears, must bring revelation under the scrutiny of an age that has a sharpened historical consciousness. Characteristically, Reinhold Niebuhr asserts, "The Christian faith begins with, and is founded upon, the affirmation that the life, death and resurrection of Christ represent an event in history. . . ."[11] The category of history has become essential for any theology that postulates that the eternal God has been revealed in Christ. "History has become our fate," says Carl Braaten, "and, like it or not, theology will persist in correlating history with revelation in one way or another."[12]

REVELATION AND HISTORY IN THE NINETEENTH CENTURY

Immanuel Kant in 1793 published *Religion Within the Limits of Reason Alone,* a short treatise which left as its legacy three options for revelation: (1) naturalism, which denies the supernatural revelation of God; (2) rationalism, which accepts historical revelation, but as only a preparatory step to the religion of reason; and (3) supernaturalism, which maintains the need for a religion revealed in a supernatural way.[13] Nineteenth-century theology was heavily influenced by Kant, devoting a large portion of its struggles to freeing itself from the confines of these three possibilities. The effort at emancipation took essentially two forms, although there were many variations.

One direction in which nineteenth-century theologians turned was toward subjective religious experience, and here the name of Friedrich Schleiermacher is most important. Although he devoted little more than a postscript to discussing revelation,[14] his whole theological system has direct bearing on the topic. Schleiermacher, influenced by Kant and German pietism, turned his attention to the human being as a knowing and feeling subject. A person, he argues, is more than just a rational and moral being, as Kant had said, but also a religious being whose highest religious experience is the feeling of absolute dependence on God. From this starting point, he proceeds to examine what he calls the human religious consciousness as he finds it expressed in the Christian community. He discovers by inductive investigation that human beings whose religious consciousness has not been awakened are in bondage to the "flesh" and stand in need of redemption. They need to be liberated in order to realize their true dependence on God. It is Jesus, as the perfect embodiment of a religious consciousness completely open to God, who becomes the redeemer—Jesus, as the supreme archetype of the human religious consciousness, makes salvation possible. The memory of Jesus, hallowed within the religious community, has efficacious influence.[15]

The significant point to note here is that Schleiermacher rests revelation neither on authoritatively communicated truths, nor on truths gleaned from speculative reason, but on the religious self-consciousness of the community. Schleiermacher sees within human experience the source of revelation, and this is what determines his basic theological conclusions. His anthropocentric presuppositions do not allow him to give primacy to history as the milieu where the event of God's self-disclosure in Jesus Christ takes place. Jesus is a perfect human being, but not the Word which has become flesh. But even though Schleiermacher finds "revelation" in the religious self-consciousness of the community, he cannot altogether escape linking revelation and history. The point where they inevitably intersect is in Jesus, who, as the supreme archetype of human religious consciousness and therefore a revelatory figure, can only be known to us "through" history.

A second response to Kant's options comes in the form of Hegel's historical dialectic. Hegel, taking his cue from Herder's historicism, locates revelation securely in history, which he defines as the process whereby the infinite Spirit comes to consciousness in the finite. Through the dialectical process of thesis, antithesis, and synthesis, God comes to self-realization. As with Schleiermacher, Hegel argues that the grasp of this divine truth of God's self-realization comes through human religious consciousness. But the apprehension is in the form of images which confuse symbol with reality, and it is the task of rational philosophy to translate these inadequate images into concepts, purging them of their merely imaginative and symbolic character. Jesus in such a framework becomes the symbol which enshrines the idea that divinity and humanity are one in essence—a necessary feature of Hegel's historical process—rather than the unique once for all and absolute revelation of God in history. In Hegel's thought, biblical emphasis is largely vitiated, but revelation remains tied to history.

Given these two options as possible ways of overcoming the hegemony of eighteenth-century rationalism, nineteenth-century theologians alternated between them. Schleiermacher's thought can be detected in varying degrees in the work of Ritschl, Hermann, Harnack, and Bousset. Following Hegel's lead were David Strauss, Ludwig Feuerbach, Alois Biedermann, and Ernst Troeltsch. Schleiermacher's emphasis on the human being as the knowing subject opened up new avenues of theological reflection which continue in full force today; yet through his followers his theology of pious self-awareness tended to degenerate into psychologism. The biblical historical drama was transformed into personal, subjective history, a product of internalization. The value of Hegel's thought was his emphasis on progressive revelation expressing itself in the particulars of history; its weakness, though, especially evident in his followers, was its denial of the unique biblical revelation of God in Christ by absorbing the event into the historical process.

There were attempts by some nineteenth-century theologians to find a mediating point between the historical and psychological poles of religious knowledge. Many thought it was possible to validate the manifestation of God in history by uniting it with genuine religious experience. Martin Kähler and Adolf Schlatter suggested such an alternative in their theology. They argued that God's revelation in history must be accompanied by its interpretation. Both the act and the word, the *Tat-Wort,* are a part of the revelation. The only Jesus we know is the Jesus whom the biblical writers wrote of as the risen Christ and Lord. They stressed both the objectivity and the suprahistorical character of the biblical *Heilsgeschichte* over against subjective religious experience and historical relativity.[16] Their efforts, however, were not as fully appreciated in their own time as they would be a generation later. They were unable to stem the tides of historicism and subjectivism. The focus of theology had shifted to the theological liberalism of Harnack and the *Religionsgeschichteschule* of Troeltsch. Historical studies which tested the uniqueness of the Christian revelation and historical relativism had become the order of the day. All philosophical ideas, religious dogmas, and moral imperatives seemed so historically conditioned or psychologically rooted that they were in danger of losing their authority. History and religious experience were proving to be difficult concepts in which to contain revelation. H. Richard Niebuhr, commenting on the relativism from which he could find no escape, notes, "No other influence has affected twentieth century thought more deeply than the discovery of spatial and temporal relativity."[17] These relativizing effects produced a kind of theological *ennui,* and the stage was set for theological change.

REVELATION AND HISTORY IN THE TWENTIETH CENTURY

The change had already been anticipated in a sort of prophetic fashion by Søren Kierkegaard who in reaction to Hegel began his discussion of revelation and history with the haunting question: "Is an historical point of departure possible for an eternal consciousness;

how can such a point of departure have any other than historical interest; is it possible to base an eternal happiness upon historical knowledge?"[18] The twentieth century rejected the notion that the personality of Jesus really could provide a solid historical foundation upon which the Christian faith could be established, as theologians of the Ritschlian period had thought. The nineteenth-century view of the Jesus of history, as Schweitzer had conclusively shown, was not the Jesus of the Bible.[19] The nineteenth-century search for the historical Jesus had presupposed that the record of the Gospels was in large part a product of the early church's imagination and theological speculation. By applying the methods of historical criticism, however, they believed that one could locate the hard core of historical facts and uncover the real Jesus who would form the foundation of Christian faith. But the rise of historical relativism changed all this; the new dialectical theologians were more inclined to echo Søren Kierkegaard's sentiment:

> If the contemporary generation had left nothing behind them but these words: "We have believed that in such and such a year God appeared among us in the humble figure of a servant, that he lived and taught in our community, and finally died," it would be more than enough.[20]

Nineteenth-century historiography, based on an immanentalist and evolutionary world view which stressed a liberal idea of progress and applied methods modeled after the natural sciences, did not provide a solid foundation for revelation.

In the first half of the twentieth century, theologians attempted to disengage Christian faith from the relativities of history without either losing the historical dimension altogether or reverting to propositional revelation. Nearly all theologians of the period related revelation to history in some fashion, but most tried to do so in a way which would free it from historical relativism.

Heading the list and representative of it in terms of influence is Karl Barth, who in dramatic fashion broke away from his theological teachers, Hermann and Harnack, and proposed that what was needed was an authentic word from God, not mere human words. Barth maintained that the ordering of the questions of theology must be determined by the framework given in divine revelation itself, not by any framework artificially imposed by human beings. His position is based on the idea that between God and the human race there exists an absolute gulf and that human beings in general are ignorant of any knowledge of God. Divine revelation must create the capacity in people to receive it. Our knowledge of God depends solely on the miracle of God's redeeming action in a Christ who forms the only bridge over the chasm. Jesus Christ, the Word of God, then, is the mediator of all knowledge of God.

Revelation makes contact by virtue of the power of the Word of God. Revelation touches history as a tangent touches a circle and provides the content of faith from above, not from history below. The Jesus of history remains elusive but real. Barth describes him as "the Rabbi of Nazareth, historically so difficult to get information about, and when it is got, one whose activity is so easily a little commonplace alongside more than one founder of a religion and alongside many later representatives of His own 'religion.'"[21] Yet Barth also later calls him

> the real and active Revealer of God and Reconciler with God, because in Him, His Son or Word, God sets and gives to be known, not some thing, be it the greatest and most significant, but Himself exactly as He posits and knows Himself from eternity and in eternity.[22]

For Barth, revelation remains related to history, but it is safely removed from its relativizing influences.

Emil Brunner places God

> outside the circle in which human knowledge and human doctrine—acquired by man's own efforts—can move, and with which they are competent to deal. Knowledge of God exists only in so far as there is a self-disclosure, a self-manifestation of God, that is, in so far as there is a "revelation."[23]

The Word has become flesh, the Eternal has entered into the sphere of historical fact, but faith alone, not historical science, can grasp it. It is only through "personal encounter"—as, for example, by means of some "I/Thou relationship"—that we can know God.

Bultmann, as a form critic, saw even more clearly what he thought to be the dangers of basing revelation on a search for the historical

Jesus. Revelation for Bultmann rests on the insight that the Scriptures are confessional documents which witness to the saving act of God. They are not a series of revealed propositions or a body of dogma, but a testimony that the object of revelation is the living God. Revelation occurs in the proclamation of the gospel (*kerygma*) when humans encounter the divine presence itself and obey God's Word in relation to their own existence. It follows that revelation comes to us in the present, not in the historical past. Bultmann does "not deny that the resurrection *kerygma* is firmly rooted to the earthly figure of the crucified Jesus"[24] yet does not see how faith can derive any support from a historical inquiry concerning him. Bultmann is careful, however, to say that without the historical figure there would be no *kerygma*.

Many contemporary theologians have not been content with so radical a separation of the Jesus of history and the Christ of faith. Gerhard Ebeling, a disciple of Bultmann's, has attempted to root the Christian revelation more firmly in the historical appearance of Jesus Christ: "revelation is primarily and properly a definite event—namely, the event attested in holy scripture—which again, to define it still more closely and state its absolute peculiarity, is the appearance of Jesus Christ."[25] He maintains that Christianity stands or falls with its connection to its historical (*historisch*) origin, "for faith is manifestly not Christian faith if it does not have a basis in the historical Jesus himself."[26]

James Barr, a dissenting voice among biblical theologians, has pointed out that while history is a necessary category for revelation it is not the only one; it has in fact, he believes, been overemphasized. He argues that positing history as the supreme milieu of God's revelation is more an apologetic effort to counter ninteteenth-century materialist, skeptical, and immanentalist philosophies than it is a biblical category.[27] Barr argues that to make the concept of history mandatory and central for revelation involves one in contradictions and antinomies. As an example, he points out that history, for the *Heilsgeschichte* theologians, is both the milieu in which God acts and the field which is described by human historical science. "Thus," he concludes,

> it is a real difficulty in many views centered in a revelation history that, in spite of a primary assertion of God's actions in history, they come to have their actual centre in historical emphasis, or a historical way of thinking, or a historical form of self-understanding or perception of life rather than in actual history.[28]

According to Barr, history has been persistently redefined and the biblical material is divided up arbitrarily to fit the appropriate theological system. Yet even Barr accepts the fact that biblical evidence, and the evidence of the Old Testament in particular, fits with and supports the assertion that "history" is the absolutely supreme milieu of God's revelation.

History and revelation have been linked in a significant way in recent thought in the theology of Wolfhart Pannenberg. For Pannenberg, revelation comes not *in* or *through* history, but *as* history.[29] To sever the *kerygma* from what really happened in history is to cut faith off from its source, for the *kerygma* is the declaration of God's acts in the affairs of humankind. The *Heilsgeschichte* theologians, according to Pannenberg, failed to show how revelation and history are really connected. Revelation, he argues, does not exist above history, entering in from outside, but is present in universal history for anyone who has eyes to see. It has been argued that the motif of revelation as a universal historical process is a relapse into Hegelianism, but Pannenberg is conscious of avoiding the dangers inherent in the Hegelian system and preserving the uniqueness of God's self-disclosure in Jesus. His concern is to overcome the cleavage between salvation history and world history by placing revelation within the universal historical process.

Other contemporary theologians from diverse traditions affirm the connection between revelation and history. Hans Küng, discussing what is special to Christianity, makes it clear that Christian faith is rooted in the coming of a historical person, Jesus of Nazareth.[30] Jürgen Moltmann makes a similar point when he speaks about the crucified Christ in the foundation and measure of Christian theology as a whole.[31] Helmut Thielicke argues that "the salvation event is part of earthly history. It is also an element in the history of religion. It can be documented as such. It is thus an object of historical science. It takes place within the world."[32] Karl Rahner links the self-communication of God firmly in history, refusing to separate the history of salvation and revelation from the whole of world history.[33] John Cobb, in developing a Christology based upon the philosophy of Whitehead, stresses the unique presence of God in Jesus in a way which does not detract from Jesus' humanity and historicity.[34]

The central conclusion that comes from this brief survey of modern views of revelation is that history is an inescapable category for revelation. "It remains true," says H. Richard Niebuhr, "that Christian faith cannot escape from partnership with history, however many other partners it may choose."[35] In fact, some statement of revelation in, through, or as history may be one unifying factor in modern theology and biblical scholarship. All who see Jesus as central to God's redemptive activity, whatever other distinctive theological emphases they may have, must figure out some way to span the two thousand years, which ultimately forces them into the problem of historical interpretation. A crucial issue, it appears, is the "use and abuse of history." This holds with special force in the all-important task of interpreting the history that surrounds the appearance of Jesus Christ, the central act of God's self-disclosure.

Faith and Historicity

The only really important traces which we have of Jesus are the documents of the New Testament. With the rise of historical thinking in the nineteenth century, it is not surprising that these documents were analyzed historically. Though many within the church viewed this critical approach to the Bible with less than favorable eyes, fearing that the results of such an analysis would be detrimental to faith, it is to the credit of Protestant Liberalism that its representatives welcomed the historical study of the Bible. Some more conservative theologians were afraid to take the risk of subjecting their understanding of the Bible to historical criticism, though in all fairness they did have some grounds for anxiety; the historical method was often bound to a closed naturalistic and positivistic world view.

After nearly two centuries of historical study of Scripture, however, it has become clear to the present generation of biblical scholarship, whether liberal or conservative, that the Bible cannot be understood outside some historical context. There can be no turning the clock back to the precritical age of biblical interpretation. As one conservative scholar has said: "These critical methods must be used because of the obvious fact that the Bible is not a magical book, but a product of history written in the words of men."[36] The historical approach to the Bible has opened our eyes to its meaning and significance in a way that was closed to ages prior to the evolution in historical thinking.

Yet when the results of applying the historical method to the Bible turned out differently from the traditional beliefs held by the church for centuries, there was cause for theological concern. As Carl Braaten suggests, there are at least three options open to the theologian:[37] (1) the historical-critical approach may be rejected outright as a valid method for interpreting the Bible, as is the case in Fundamentalism; (2) there may be a declaration of peaceful co-existence made in which both history and faith are given their respective domains, a course followed by many theologians of the modern era, and perhaps most notably by Rudolf Bultmann; (3) there may be an attempt to integrate both the historical and theological disciplines. It is this latter approach that seems to have the best possibility of doing justice to Christian revelation.

Option one, the rejection of the historical-critical approach to the interpretation of the Bible seems an unlikely route for theology to pursue. Even if one maintains that the Bible is the infallibly written Word of God, it still must be admitted that this Word of God is given to human beings through historical events and historical personages. This very fact demands historical criticism, and historical criticism, it should be remembered, is theologically neutral. It need not rule out by definition the possibility of God's intervention in history. Historical criticism of the Bible simply means making intelligent judgments about the evidence, not deciding *a priori* what can happen in history.

The second option, the separation between history and faith, is epitomized by Rudolf Bultmann's call to demythologize the New Testament by means of an existential interpretation. Bultmann's concern is to avoid the inevitable collision between historical fact and existential faith by placing faith out of reach of historical scrutiny and by attempting a redefinition of history. He maintains that the best approach to understanding the New Testament message is not in recovering historical facts, but in recognizing that the New Testament has mythological elements. It was written at a time far enough removed from the history it records to lose touch with the actual situation, and thus its authors have imposed their prescientific world view on its pages. A reconstruction is necessary on the basis of the critical principles of historical study. But faith does not need to wait for the answers uncovered by historical reconstruction. What is important in the New Testament message is human self-understanding. By demythologizing the New Testament this essential message becomes clear. The real issue for faith is not what happened *then* but what happens *now* in the moment of existential decision. It is the Christ of faith, not the Jesus of history, with whom we are concerned. The meaning of the *kerygma* is not to be sought in uncovering the historical Jesus, which is impossible anyway, but in the awareness of responsibility before God. Brute facts, uncovered by disinterested and objective history, are unimportant for faith. Bultmann does not deny that they exist, only that they are not essential for faith. There is a different level of historical knowledge which is important for faith, and that is existential knowledge through encounter with history. The meaning of history is to be sought in the present because "every historical moment has its own meaning in itself in that it implies openness to God and that it has the possibility of becoming the eschatological moment."[38] As Bultmann expresses it: "The meaning of history lies always in the present; and when the present is conceived as the eschatological present by Christian faith, the meaning of history is realized."[39]

Such a redefinition of history may have eased some tensions, but it has created others also. In the theology of the last decade there has been a gradual consensus that the chasm between faith and history must somehow be spanned. Few theologians would deny their indebtedness to Bultmann's thought, but few also are completely at ease with his nearly total divorce of the *kerygma* from history. Gerhard Ebeling, though he stands squarely in the Bultmannian tradition, states: "Christianity stands or falls with the tie that binds it to its unique historical origin."[40]

The theology of Wolfhart Pannenberg, as has been suggested, is an expression of this dissatisfaction over the split between faith and history. It most dramatically represents option three, the effort to unite the historical and theological disciplines. Pannenberg wants to emancipate historical method from its "Babylonian captivity" to positivism and naturalism. He argues that to retreat to the security of traditional dogma (e.g., Karl Barth) or existential decision (e.g., Rudolf Bultmann) is to dodge the issue. If revelation is historical occurrence, then the historical method should be an appropriate way of uncovering it.

In order to accomplish this, historical methodology must be freed from its anthropocentric presuppositions. The principles of research do not necessarily imply that human beings rather than God are the moving force behind history. Though Pannenberg is careful to acknowledge that historical science is a human effort and one which makes use of analogy, he nonetheless argues that this does not necessarily preclude the possibility of the novel and unrepeatable. The historian should not deny the possibility of an event simply because there is no immediate analogy to it in the everyday experience of reality. Faith and history are brought together in Pannenberg's view by his concept of revelation *as* history.[41] God stands behind all history, giving it all meaning, not just one particular segment. For "only from the vantage point of universal history is it possible to find the complete meaning of any single event."[42] Without this postulate, history is a meaningless maze of occurrences. He says: "The unity of history can . . . only be understood in a way in which its connection and contingency have a common root."[43] The totality of reality as history is God's world which God created and through which God is revealed. The living God of the Bible is Lord over all nations, not just Israel. Because God's revelation to humankind comes as history, the historical method is the only reliable way of dealing with the past, and faith must be content to be at least partially dependent on the results of historical research. In fact, historical reason and faith are not inseparable acts following a chronological or psychological sequence but coessential dimensions of the total act of the person. Pannenberg's concern is to reverse the subjectivistic emphasis in theology which has thrived since Schleiermacher and which holds that revelation derives from the experience of faith rather than from reason's knowledge of history. When the role of reason is removed from the act of faith, nothing prevents faith from postulating whatever is emotionally satisfying. He even refuses to separate historical knowledge from saving faith. For Pannenberg, there can be no split between the two.

Pannenberg's radical departure from the neo-Kantian distinction between reality and value and his new emphasis on the historicity of the saving events are to be welcomed, as is his straightforward effort to free historiography from the confines of its naturalistic presuppositions and his bold attempt to reunite reason and faith. His work has opened up whole new vistas for theological reflection. Yet there are points where his theology seems vulnerable to criticism.[44]

In the first place, he fails to do justice to the doctrine of the Word of God. The place of the *kerygma* as the mediator of the historical revelation tends to be diminished. He defines God's revelation as merely a matter of historical facts; it is *there* for anyone who has eyes to see. Secondly, because of this position he almost substitutes sight for faith. Faith for Pannenberg becomes not so much a gift of the Spirit of God as it is a product of reason. There seems little room left for trust. Finally, he seems to lose the category of uniqueness in the redemptive events. Although one appreciates his effort to keep faith which is not based on fact from entering the picture, it does not follow that there can be no unique and special revelation. Just because God is seen as the prime mover in all historical events does not necessarily imply that the divine presence is not revealed in a special way at particular times and places. These points of vulnerability, though, do not diminish the gains made in emancipating Christian theology from the bondage of positivistic assumptions in historiography.

The problem of the relationship between faith and history has again raised the issue of the historical Jesus. The historical-critical approach, built on positivistic assumptions, originally met its greatest obstacle in its attempt to isolate the historical Jesus. The field of biblical scholarship is cluttered with failures to explain who Jesus of Nazareth was and what his meaning is for us.[45] With the rise of historical thinking in the nineteenth century, the traditional christological formulations were seriously challenged. The unqualified acceptance of the Chalcedonian model was undermined when it was demonstrated that there was dependence on Greek philosophical categories. It was thought that Jesus as he "really" was had been buried in a theological system of abstract concepts. The Jesus of the Gospels and the Christ of the creeds appeared to be quite different. Even among the laity there was a genuine suspicion that Jesus had been misunderstood.

This shift from dogmatic to historical perspective culminated in an intensive effort to reconstruct an authentic replica of Jesus. The scholars of this era made a sincere effort to rid themselves of their theological presuppositions in order to uncover the core of historical reality about Jesus. Yet preunderstanding, as we demonstrated in chapter one, is not so easily shed; and between the lines of the assorted biographies of Jesus the cultural and religious viewpoints of their authors may be discerned. What was historically discovered during that time more often than not corresponded in perhaps too convenient a fashion to what was needed theologically.

In general, the "quest for the historical Jesus" was divided between naturalistic and supernaturalistic approaches, with the majority being "positive" in that they attempted to establish faith on a solid historical foundation. Among the "negative" and more radical attempts to reconstruct a picture of Jesus was the attempt of David Strauss. He argued that the historical life of Jesus was hidden beneath a thick layer of religious mythology. Being a radical Hegelian, he was not particularly bothered about this reduction of historical content in the Gospels but was concerned with the notion that the essence of Christianity is to be found in the idea of God-humanhood which entered historical consciousness for the first time in Jesus. The idea once launched, argued Strauss, no longer needed the undergirding for genuine evidence of a historical event to demonstrate its validity.

Ultimately, it was the rigorous application of the historical method itself which signaled the defeat of the attempt to reconstruct a true portrait of the historical Jesus. Albert Schweitzer's study of the "life-of-Jesus" movement and his conclusive argument that the eschatological preaching of Jesus conflicts with modern notions of religion and morality marked the end of the era. Schweitzer writes: "Thus each successive epoch of theology found its own thoughts in Jesus; that was, indeed, the only way in which it could make him live."[46] At the beginning of the twentieth century the frustrating presence of irreconcilable viewpoints produced a general historical skepticism, and the way was opened for a new theological approach.

In the latter part of the nineteenth century the theologian Martin Kähler maintained that the only Jesus whom we know is the one preached as the risen Christ who is Lord. In his book *The So-Called Historical Jesus and the Historic, Biblical Christ,* he argued that the real Christ is not "the historical Jesus" but the "kerygmatic Christ." Kähler was repudiating not the earthly Jesus but the Jesus who had been manufactured by the historiography of the nineteenth century. What was needed, he asserted, was the Christ of the Bible who lived, died, and rose again from the dead.

It was into this general framework that the dialectical theologians of the 1920s and 30s moved. Reacting against the mood of historical skepticism, they attempted to free Christology from its dependence on the historical and psychological pictures of the personality of Jesus. Influenced by Søren Kierkegaard, who had argued that historical inquiry into the life of Jesus can never produce anything certain or relevant for faith, people such as Barth, Brunner, Gogarten, Tillich, and Bultmann all disclaimed the historical Jesus movement.

The problem raised for theology by this disclaimer on the quest for the historical Jesus was whether any break between faith and historical research could be tolerated. Reaction to this problem is evident in the theology of Rudolf Bultmann. Bultmann accepted Kähler's idea that the Gospels are kerygmatic witnesses to Christ and not biographical reports. True faith therefore rests on the *kerygma,* not on the shaky foundation of historical research. Yet Bultmann does not seem quite willing to rely on this assertion completely. He maintains that at least the bare fact of Jesus' historicity, and his death on the cross, are themselves necessary to this *kerygma*.[47] But if the *kerygma* is dependent at all on Jesus then faith cannot be independent of historical inquiry. This inconsistency in Bultmann's theology has its root in his uncritical acceptance of the positivist historiography of the nineteenth century. His acceptance of the presuppositions of this view of history forces Bultmann to remove faith from historical inquiry and root it in existential categories. Yet he retains the factuality of Jesus' life and death, though somewhat inconsistently, in order to maintain some connection between Jesus and the *kerygma*.

In more recent theology, the tendency to accept the conclusion that the historical Jesus bears little or no relationship to faith has gradually eroded. Joachim Jeremias writes:

> To anyone who is not aware of the controversy, the question whether the historical Jesus and his messages have any significance for the Christian faith must sound absurd. No one in the ancient church, no one in the church of the Reformation period and the two succeeding centuries thought of asking such a question.[48]

There is a new openness to the possibility, even necessity, of uniting faith and history in some meaningful fashion. Another New Testament scholar summarizes the situation as follows:

> Today, however, we can be grateful that neither the rarefied atmosphere of the "theology of the Word" and of "existentialist theology," nor the impasse reached by criticism, have stifled the breath of continuing empirical concern to investigate and shed light on the concrete historical character of the revelation in the man Jesus of Nazareth.[49]

There is the growing conviction that "to hold a historical faith is to have a faith which stands or falls with the records."[50] Stephen Neill remarks: "It seems to be the case that the faith of the Church stands or falls with the general reliability of the historical evidence for the life and death of Jesus Christ."[51] The Dutch theologian, Hendrikus Berkhof, concludes that "what we believe and confess concerning Christ as the meaning of history is related to the reality with which our history books are concerned."[52]

This concern to explore the relationship between the historical Jesus and the *kerygma* has been labeled "the new quest of the historical Jesus."[53] The common concern of the movement (not so new anymore) is to establish the correspondence between history and proclamation. In calling for a new quest there is no devaluation of the enormity of the problem. There is a general recognition that the same difficulties and limitations in researching Jesus obtain now as did in earlier efforts. The historian is still subject to the negative influence of presuppositions; and there is no documentary evidence from Jesus' contemporaries of an objective character upon which to build a neutral portrait of Jesus. There is also the general acknowledgment, to which Pannenberg is a notable exception, that historical research cannot begin with facts, even interpreted facts, and go on to tell us about the revelatory and redemptive action of God.[54]

Günther Bornkamm is representative of this new quest. In his study of Jesus, he writes:

> No one is any longer in a position to write a life of Jesus [because] . . . we possess no single word of Jesus and no single story of Jesus, no matter how incontestably genuine they may be, which do not contain at the same time the confession of the believing congregation or at least are embedded therein. This makes the search after the bare facts of history difficult and to a large extent futile.[55]

Yet a few pages later, he manages to justify his own effort when he says: "Although the Gospels do not speak of the history of Jesus in the way of reproducing the course of his career in all its happenings and stages, in its inner and outer development, nevertheless they do speak of history as occurrence and event."[56]

Ernst Fuchs[57] and Gerhard Ebeling[58] have turned their inquiries into a specific theological program. Working closely together they have developed a hermeneutical theory which rests upon the relationship between language and faith. The historical Jesus and the kerygmatic Christ are linked together in the concept of the word-event. These theologians are not specifically interested in a biographical account of Jesus, but instead, what uniquely came to expression in him—namely, faith. To believe in Jesus means to reenact the decision of faith which Jesus originally evoked. Jesus is more the witness to faith than he is the object of faith. His historicity is nevertheless important, for, as Ebeling puts it, "faith is manifestly not Christian faith if it does not have a basis in the historical Jesus Himself."[59] He further argues that "if the quest of the historical Jesus were in fact to prove that faith in Jesus has no basis in Jesus himself, then that would be the end of Christology."[60]

Other theologians less influenced by Bultmann have welcomed the new quest as a justification of their original positions—that interest in the historical Jesus was a legitimate theological concern. Theologians like Joachim Jeremias, Oscar Cullmann, and Ethelbert Stauffer have really never bowed to Bultmann's prohibitions on searching beyond the *kerygma* for historical fact in order to more firmly root faith.

It is beyond the scope of this study to discuss the new quest in its many forms in greater detail. Our purpose is rather to report the general consensus, even among the Bultmannian theologians, that there is a continuity between Jesus and the *kerygma*. There must be at least a minimum core of factuality regarding Jesus if the *kerygma* is to present us with a way of life that is realistic and not culled from a dream world.[61] This factual element can and should be treated by the historical-critical approach, for, as Alan Richardson reminds us, "The affirmations of the Christian creeds are historical, not metaphysical, in character, and Christian theology itself is a matter of the interpretation of history."[62]

Faith and the Resurrection of Christ

For two reasons, the particular affirmation of the Christian creeds around which the Jesus of history/Christ of faith debate centers is the resurrection. In the first place, if there is one issue on which the biblical scholars are agreed in their study of the earliest Christian traditions, it is that faith in the risen Christ forms an indispensable part of the *kerygma;* it is the heart of the Christian faith. The second reason involves one of the most important developments in recent biblical studies: the discovery that the resurrection has a degree of resistibility to hypotheses that fail to reckon with its historicity.[63]

Ironically, though there is a widely held consensus that the resurrection forms an essential part of the *kerygma,* many divergent scholars and theologians, despite their differences, agree that the resurrection is not a historical event. They look for continuity in Jesus' faith, in his preaching, his idea of grace, his attitudes, actions, or self-understanding, but not in his resurrection. The mere fact that there is such a wide acceptance of Bultmann's remark that "an historical event which involves a resurrection from the dead is utterly inconceivable"[64] is remarkable in itself. Why do positions on both the right and left of Bultmann share this view that the event of the resurrection forms no part of the historical problem of the life of Jesus?

The answer lies in the acceptance of a naturalistic view of history, a position which involves these theologians in affirming the centrality of the resurrection as an event of past history. In an attempt to maintain continuity with the *kerygma* of the early church they are thus forced to maintain its meaning while denying its historical reality—a point of view not easily convincing. For example, Bultmann sustains this position by means of his familiar existential interpretation. Because the resurrection accounts are not statements about what really happened but expressions of faith in the New Testament community, they may be retained in the symbolic language of faith as the expression of self-understanding. But can a historical approach to the resurrection be ignored in the consideration of the life of Jesus question? Is it possible to really understand Jesus apart from the resurrection?

In the 1950s there began to appear a series of studies that urged theology to move toward accepting the historicity of Christ's resurrection.[65] These volumes have attempted to show that the resurrection accounts have an early place in the development of the tradition and hence are acceptable as authentic historical reports. In the 1960s other volumes appeared, and of special note are Wolfhart Pannenberg's *Jesus-God and Man* (1964) and Jürgen Moltmann's *Theology of Hope* (1964) in which there is a scholarly effort to place the historical resurrection of Jesus at the center of the theology of the church. All of these scholars describe the resurrection as a historical event without denying its existential meaning. For them there is an indispensable unity of event and meaning.

For both Pannenberg and Moltmann the issue hinges on the preunderstanding that is brought to the historical task. It all depends on what is meant by the concept of history. For Pannenberg, "it is the close examination of the reports of the resurrection that determines its historicity, and not the prior judgment that all events in history must be more or less the same."[66] Moltmann has concentrated on showing how the modern preunderstanding of what is historically possible stands in direct conflict with the biblical view of what is historically possible.[67] The Bible understands historical possibility in terms of the activity of God, and it is an openness to the possibility of God's intervention for which we have been arguing. For as one scholar concludes, "nothing is to be gained by coming to the New Testament already strongly prejudiced against any possibility that God could have raised Jesus from the dead, as an event in our world and in our time."[68] It is not necessary to maintain with Bornkamm that "the event of Christ's resurrection . . .[is] removed from historical scholarship."[69] In order to do justice to the resurrection, there must be a rejection of all ready-made answers. Whether an event happened or not cannot be settled before the fact. The fact of whether Christ rose from the dead is an exceedingly difficult problem to resolve. One must ask all sort of theological questions, including the meaning of the resurrection and whether there is or need be a resurrection apart from faith. But faith in the resurrection also raises the historical question, and this question must be answered by interpreting the evidence.

It is not our purpose to go into the nature of the evidence for Christ's resurrection, but a brief comment on the issues involved in judging it may be helpful. There are two basic criteria for evaluating and interpreting historical evidence: (1) the rigorous application of the historical method itself which insures as far as possible the objectivity of the facts; and (2) the preunderstanding of the historian. Applying these two criteria to the resurrection involves then both the examination of the attestations of the witnesses to see if what is recorded could be more rationally accounted for by some alternative hypothesis, and the maintenance of a preunderstanding checked by the historical-critical approach which remains open and sympathetic to the message of that evidence.[70]

The evidence available to us concerning Christ's resurrection involves the Easter traditions handed down by the early church. These resurrection narratives, arising from the community which came into being for the express purpose of being a witness to the resurrection, constitute the primary evidence for it. What is needed is a careful analysis of the two strands of the tradition, one dealing with the appearances of the risen Lord and the other with the phenomenon of the empty tomb.[71] Today there is a great deal more openness to the historical reliability of the resurrection testimonies. Even the tradition of the empty tomb is not easily dismissed as having no authentic historical content.

Although the results of biblical scholarship may not lead us to faith in the risen Lord, they at least clear the way for it by removing false hindrances. The historian's ability to accept the resurrection will ultimately depend on the preunderstanding which is brought to the evidence. Alan Richardson's point that "the historian's final judgment of the evidence will, then, in the last report and after as vigorous a critical appraisal as he can make, be determined by the man he is,"[72] is well taken. The gulf of time between the historian and the object of study must be bridged from both ends. The evidence must be carefully analyzed, and the historian's mind must be open to receive the truth of the event in question.

"Hearing" the Word of God

What conclusions can be drawn from this discussion of modern views of revelation, history, and faith? A first certainly is that Christian faith is linked to history; another is that a central affirmation of faith, the resurrection of Jesus, cannot be easily discounted as nonhistorical. Further, the historian must be free of preconceived ideas that preclude the possibility that God can be an active agent in history, causing, for example, the resurrection to occur. Finally, and more positively, to believe that God is an active agent in history, one will have to have a preunderstanding that is open to accepting the implications of the evidence. This point holds equally for the believer as well as one who comes to the biblical material doubting its authenticity. But in the case of an "event" such as the resurrection one will have to know in one's own life something of the experience of the church as it worships Jesus as the living Lord. In short, one will have to have faith as a rational motive for affirming that Jesus is the risen Lord.

Faith, then, is the necessary preunderstanding for the interpretation of the Christian faith. In maintaining that the revelation is inextricably tied to history we have also committed ourselves to the historical method as a second necessary ingredient for an adequate preunderstanding. Faith is firmly rooted in historical probability, though it is born not of historical knowledge but of God. Historical evidence may suggest that God is present and acting in the events of history, but it cannot supply the personal experience of trust in and commitment to the risen Lord. Yet such evidence will prevent faith from postulating anything it wishes. Thus faith and historical study are not basically opposed to each other; they necessarily intersect in Jesus Christ and constitute the minimum requirements for a hermeneutical approach to the Christian revelation. Faith and historical study allow us to hear the Word of God.

SUGGESTED READING

Anderson, Hugh. *Jesus and Christian Origins*. Oxford: Oxford University, 1964.

Aulén, Gustaf. *Jesus in Contemporary Historical Research*. Philadelphia: Fortress, 1976.

Baillie, John. *The Idea of Revelation in Recent Thought*. Oxford: Oxford University, 1956.

Berkhof, Hendrikus. *Christ and the Meaning of History*. London: SCM, 1966.

Jeremias, Joachim. *The Problem of the Historical Jesus*. Philadelphia: Fortress, 1964.

Marxsen, Willi. *The Resurrection of Jesus of Nazareth*. Philadelphia: Fortress, 1970.

Moltmann, Jürgen. *The Theology of Hope*. New York: Harper and Row, 1967.

Niebuhr, H. Richard. *The Meaning of Revelation*. New York: Macmillan, 1962.

Pannenberg, Wolfhart. *Revelation as History*. New York: Macmillan, 1968.

Robinson, James M., and John B. Cobb, Jr., eds. *Theology as History*. New York: Harper and Row, 1967.

II

The Practice of Hermeneutics

Once the interpreter has clarified the issues of biblical hermeneutics it is possible to move with more confidence to the text. As one does so, one is immediately faced with the responsibility of finding an adequate methodology, of coping with the variety of writings, and of using the Bible in the service of the church.

4
Finding a Method

The Present Situation

In order to handle the text fairly and accurately, the interpreter of Scripture must have a thorough understanding of the nature of the Bible and be clear about the role that assumptions about the Bible and its message will have on the interpretive product. It is also essential that the interpreter is aware of the variety of methodological options available and the impact that any choice of method will have on the outcome of the interpretive effort.

One would think, after the amount of time and energy which has been devoted to the study of Scripture, there would be a consensus among biblical scholars about methodology. But consensus on methodology, as with a guiding hermeneutical principle, is not so easy to achieve, especially after the partial disaffection which has recently set in about the historical-critical approach. The extreme conservative wing of the church has never had great affection for the historical-critical approach, but in the last several years even those who were its most able proponents and practitioners have begun to ask some questions regarding its viability.[1]

The questions have in general come from those who are eager to preserve the canon as the Scriptures of the church and from those who sincerely believe it is possible to build a theology for the church on top of a thorough historical-critical approach to the Bible. Dissatisfaction has come with the inability to find a way to formulate a theology out of the historical-critical approach, with the result that the Bible and theology have all too frequently been separated. Biblical scholars, like their counterparts in virtually every other academic field, have been consistently more adept at deconstruction than reconstruction, which is to say that they were able to analyze the text in terms of its origin and function but less able to draw theological insight from the text to guide the church. Biblical theology has not spoken with great influence on the relationship of the gospel to the world, nor have the themes of biblical theology really penetrated the life of the church, imparting styles of Christian living, guidance for worship and hymnology, a solid foundation for preaching and pastoral care, and direction for the church's mission in the world.

It is certainly not possible to go back to a precritical era, ignoring the enormous progress which has been made in biblical scholarship over the last century, although there are reputable scholars who "come close" to advocating such a position.[2] The better approach, though, seems to be in the direction of utilizing the understanding of the Bible which the critical approach has provided and finding better ways of preserving the Bible as the Scripture of the church. It is to this purpose that the present chapter is devoted.

Getting Oriented

Textbooks on the subject of biblical hermeneutics often divide the discussion into general and special hermeneutics,[3] the former being devoted to basic principles about context, language, history, and culture. Special hermeneutics refers to the study of the variety of uses of language and genre which occur in the Bible, including figures of speech, typology, symbol, poetry, prophecy, and doctrinal teaching. It also refers to the study of appropriate uses of Scripture in preaching, worship, and Christian nurture. We will discuss "general" hermeneutics here and then turn to "special" hermeneutics in succeeding chapters.

CONTEXT

A primary concern of the interpreter is understanding the context of the passage to be interpreted. In some passages of Scripture an understanding of the context is of lesser importance, but on the whole knowing how the context delineates and defines the text is necessary to a fair and accurate interpretation of it.

The study of context enables the interpreter to understand the line of thought of the writer. There are places in Scripture where the material has been merely collected and little relationship between units (pericopes) is evident; in other places the author may make a swift departure from the pursued train of thought. But whether the ideas are bound together by a tightly woven argument or the connections are more distant, the meaning of a particular passage is nearly always controlled in part by what precedes and what follows it.

The *immediate* context of a passage—the few paragraphs which precede and follow—provides the best clues about the meaning of the passage. Originally there were no verses or chapter divisions, so that the interpreter should not be too strictly bound by an adherence to English Bible designations. These may be helpful, but they do not always represent the best boundary lines.

The larger context, the entire chapter or book, also provides valuable clues to the meaning of a passage. In the writings of Paul, for example, there is often a logic which unfolds from beginning to end, and no single passage or paragraph can be easily understood apart from the whole. Another part of the larger context is the presence of parallel passages in other books of the Bible. This is particularly apparent in the Gospels, where different accounts are given of incidents in the life of Jesus.

In Scripture where context is less important, such as the Wisdom literature of the Old Testament (e.g., Proverbs), there is still value in understanding how the editor has arranged the material. The same principle applies in the New Testament where in the Gospels, for instance, the evangelists also serve as editors and collectors of material and frequently have arranged the material by subject matter.

LANGUAGE

The study of the philosophy of language, linguistics, linguistical theory, and the details of grammar are beyond our scope here, but an appreciation of the basic elements of language usage in the Bible is essential to the interpreter.

It is easy to forget that the biblical languages were used far more in their oral than in their written form. The oral forms of Hebrew, Aramaic, and Greek were probably more important to the people of biblical times than the oral form of each language today, for they had high illiteracy, few books, and no newspapers, and thus communication was more often than not confined to speech. The sounds and pronunciations of the words of these languages are in part lost to us, but there is no doubt that a good deal was communicated by sound (*phonemes*).

The forms of words (*morphology*) are even more crucial than sound in determining meaning. The biblical languages are highly inflected, with tense, mood, voice, person, and number all influencing the particular form used. The meaning of a passage often becomes much clearer upon a careful examination of the specific form chosen by an author.[4]

The meaning of words (*lexicography*) is also of vital importance in deciphering the precise meaning of a text. A number of valuable tools which summarize the results of careful research are available to the interpreter in this regard.[5] Some acquaintance with the root meaning of words (*etymology*) and the usage of words in particular contexts and eras of history can also add greatly to the richness of the interpretation, although some caution should be exercised in overanalyzing root meanings. There is a tendency on the part of some interpreters to stress the etymology of words and neglect the fact that the original users of the words were in most cases unaware of the root meanings, that they were in fact merely assigning the same concretized meaning to the words which they had learned within their culture.

A careful study of how words are related to each other (*syntax*) may also shed light on the meaning of a text. Syntax is essentially the study of thought relations, and in order to accurately understand the thought patterns of the author, the interpreter must give attention to the syntactical relationships. A recent development in the study of syntax is the increasing interest in "codes" in the biblical language which point to certain esoteric significations. There is a general acknowledgment that the language of a living religious faith (which surely applies to the people of ancient Israel and the early Christian community) is full of sign and symbol. Such language is judged for syntactic adequacy by reference to its own internal language norms. It is also judged for mystery, poetry, satisfying profundity, and even oddness, which is characteristic of all religious utterance and which points to the transcendence of God.

HISTORY AND CULTURE

For well over a century, the use of a refined historical method has been the standard tool box of all serious interpreters of the Bible. Without a knowledge of the history and culture of biblical times, the interpreter may inadvertently impose an alien point of view onto the text, distorting its meaning.

In the next section of this chapter there will be a more detailed account of the specific techniques that are used in examining the Bible historically. It is important here to note, however, the value of a general historical awareness for the fair and accurate interpretation of the Scriptures, beginning with a working knowledge of the geography and archaeology of the area. To know the land where the events occurred and the way of life of the people is basic. A study of the political situation of the Near East in biblical times and how it shaped the life of the people can put many of the events of Scripture into an understandable context.

To know something of the material conditions of the people—their homes, family patterns, means of transportation, state of the economy, and the relative role of agriculture—may bring out shades of meaning in a passage that might not be apparent otherwise. The pattern of social relationships, the religious beliefs, the values, and the differences between urban and rural life may also include factors that reveal the more subtle dimensions of a text. In short, a thorough grasp of the history and culture of biblical times is of great value to the interpreter of the Bible and increases the probability that an accurate interpretation of the text will be rendered. This assertion in no way implies that interpreters of Scripture in the first eighteen hundred years of the church were unable to discern the meaning of the biblical passages with which they worked. But the work of the best of them might have been improved had they had a better understanding of some of these historical factors.

Biblical Criticism

A number of historical approaches to Scripture have been developed which go beyond an acquaintance with the context, languages, history, and culture of biblical times. These approaches may in the broadest sense be classified as biblical criticism.[6] They represent a comparing, a contrasting, and an analyzing response to the biblical literature with the stated goal of discerning the meaning of the text.

In biblical studies the word "criticism" does not imply captious faultfinding or a conscious effort to undermine the authority of Scripture. It is rather used in the etymological sense of distinguishing, deciding, judging, or coming to an informed opinion. The process is essentially a rational reflection on the data which are supplied by historical inquiry. It has no destructive intent and should in no way be viewed as "dangerous" to the well-being of the church. It is true, however, that a critical approach to the Bible will yield different results than a dogmatic approach which rejects any critical scrutiny. If one views the Bible as inspired throughout and as an infallible guide on all subjects with which it deals, there will be one interpretive result; if the interpreter is informed by critical historical analysis, however, there will be another. Methodology is as much a preunderstanding as is one's theological orientation.

Regardless of assumptions, though, a fundamental maxim of biblical interpretation (exegesis) is that the interpreter must be subservient to the text itself—that is, the interpreter must allow the text to determine its interpretation. In order to understand the text the interpreter must "stand under," listen to, and hear the text and not impose a foreign meaning onto it. Biblical criticism (the historical-critical approach) is designed to further such interpretation; first by establishing a certain objective distance between the interpreter and the passage, but secondly, oddly enough, by also drawing the interpreter of Scripture into the text, into the position of its first readers. Biblical literature "comes through" to the interpreter as a message from another culture—that of ancient Israel and the early church. The literature preserves its status as a foreign document with its strangeness, its particularity, and uniqueness. But the interpreter is also emphatically drawn into the drama itself, whereby the far-off scenes and events take on an apparent immediacy. The impact of the words are felt with a startling directness. Thus biblical criticism commits the interpreter to having both distance and intimacy with the biblical passage.

As valuable as the historical and philological tools are, though, they are not the only ones necessary for biblical interpretation within the context of the church. Historical analysis, which attempts to accurately reconstruct the past, blends into exegesis, which has as its purpose the drawing out the meaning of the text. Then the theologians have the important responsibility of reflecting on the meaning of the text in order to provide guidance for the church and for those who minister within the church on a day-to-day basis. Most importantly, it is the task of those who preach and teach to interpret the Scriptures in a way which nurtures and guides the people of God.

TEXTUAL CRITICISM

There is no *necessary* order in the task of biblical criticism, but finding and utilizing the best available text is perhaps the best place to start. Textual criticism, often called lower criticism, is concerned with comparing various witnesses to the early text of a document; its goal is to establish the most accurate text. There is an abundance of manuscripts and other important data which may be used to get back to a very early period in the New Testament transmission. For example, the Greek text of the New Testament found in the twenty-sixth edition of the *Novum Testamentum Graece,* the most popular handbook edition of the New Testament, contains approximately two thousand five hundred variants from the reading given by any one of the typical ancient manuscripts. Likewise, the gap in the transmission of the Old Testament, once considerable, has been substantially reduced since the discovery of the Dead Sea Scrolls, although the textual problems in the Old Testament are far more complex and numerous than those in the New Testament. Nonetheless, it is the textual critic who attempts to analyze the multitude of texts available and discern which text is most likely closest to the original—or to put it another way, to ascertain the "correct" reading of the text. Fortunately, the difficult and complex work of the textual critic results in a "preferred text" which is available to the interpreter who therefore need not necessarily become greatly involved in the technical work of textual criticism.

LITERARY CRITICISM

Literary criticism attempts to establish the meaning of a text by studying its historical and literary environment. This approach involves a whole range of concerns and is often called higher criticism.

Attention in higher criticism is given to problems of authorship, authenticity, collaboration, revision, chronology, genre, and even such details as word usage, sentence structure, and paragraph construction. Because of the wide range of concerns grouped under the rubric "literary criticism," the term does carry some ambiguity.

For example, some would argue that literary criticism is primarily concerned with the sources making up the biblical document. Others understand literary criticism to be the study which seeks to discern the author's intention by means of an analysis of the text's structure and component elements. Still others use the category of literary criticism to refer to methods currently employed in the study of contemporary literature, finding elements in the New Testament, for example, of comedy and tragedy. The traditional and most widely accepted usage of the term, however, continues to be the study of the sources which have contributed to the final form of the biblical document, a methodology referred to as *source criticism*.

SOURCE CRITICISM

The objectives of source criticism are threefold: (1) to trace the development of the document, observing how various sources contributed to the document's final form; (2) to evaluate its historical accuracy in light of the historical development of the document; and (3) to determine how various biblical documents may be interdependent. For example, in the Old Testament the division of the Pentateuch into J, E, D, and P sources has helped biblical interpreters to understand the purposes of specific sections of these first five books of the Old Testament. In the New Testament, source criticism has centered in the Synoptics, although it is not limited to them. Source criticism has close ties with redaction criticism (see below), which focuses on editorial usage and on specific modifications made by the author who introduces source material into the work. The concern of source criticism is at once literary, historical, and theological. It is literary in its desire to discover how each of the books of the New Testament was composed; it is historical in its interest in the history of the early Christian church which the sources help to unravel; and it is certainly theological in its attempt to compare the theology of the sources and that of the extant documents.[7]

The methodology employed by the source critic is straightforward enough, though it does involve some careful detective work. The evidence which is examined is of two types: internal and external. Sometimes a book of the Bible will give either direct or indirect information concerning its authorship, date, origin, destination, composition, and intention. At other times, these factors are more difficult to determine by internal means, and the critic is forced to make use of the external evidence found in the historical circumstances surrounding the document or in references found in ancient church traditions and writings contemporaneous with the biblical literature. Primary importance is placed on the internal evidence, which frequently supports the external evidence but at times seems to conflict with it. Criteria utilized in choosing between conflicting reports are redundancy, context, vocabulary, style, and ideology. The result of this effort is the reconstruction of the story of the document—what happened, how and when it happened, and why.

FORM CRITICISM

Form criticism is a more specialized approach to biblical interpretation concerned with analyzing folk material. It might be described as the analysis of typical forms through which human experience is verbally expressed. Whereas textual, literary, and source criticisms all examine a book of the New Testament as a written document (of which several divergent editions may exist), form criticism treats each book of the New Testament as an expression of human experience with its own special history. Manifest to us in human language, the books of the New Testament are subject to the laws of communication which govern human experience. Underlying this approach are the premises that folk memory both is the primary vehicle of tradition and is preserved in small units. Isolating these irreducible units (*forms*) of the primitive tradition and discovering their usage in the life of a community (*life situation*) have the potential of revealing how the Bible came to be in its present form.

Again this method has been used primarily in dealing with the Synoptic Gospels, although it is not inherently limited to them. Biblical scholars largely responsible for the refinement of the method are Martin Dibelius and Rudolf Bultmann. Dibelius, in his analysis of tradition units (*pericopes*), suggests five "forms": paradigm, *Novelle,* legend, parenesis, and myth. Of these paradigm is the most important. Paradigm is defined by Dibelius as those concise, self-contained, and edifying stories which focus on the significant sayings and deeds of Jesus. Their power lay in their persistent usage by the church in its preaching ministry. The other forms were also carefully analyzed by Dibelius in terms of their function in the life of the early church. Bultmann's main contribution to the field is his *History of the Synoptic Tradition* (1921) in which he systematically sorts all the material of these three Gospels into classifications of forms, many of which overlap. Bultmann's work was to have a profound influence on subsequent New Testament scholarship.[8]

REDACTION CRITICISM

Redaction criticism, partially in reaction to radical consequences obtained in applying the form-critical method, attempts to discern what theological motifs were used by the biblical authors in arranging and modifying the material they received. Since the form-critical approach tended to undercut the personality and intention of the authors, the redaction critic focuses instead on the author's apparent purpose and on the editorial process itself. Some scholars recognized that the evangelists of the Gospels were not mere collectors and transmitters of traditional material, as the form critics claimed, but redactors (editors and revisers). They arranged and altered the material they received to express their own theology or that of the church of their day—a theology occasionally quite different from that of the original.[9]

As a methodology for New Testament study, redaction criticism attempts to clarify the nature and extent of the author's own contribution to the work. It presupposes literary, source, and form criticism but moves on to determine how the New Testament authors collected, arranged, and edited traditional material in a particular set of circumstances with a specific objective in mind. In order to make this determination redaction criticism examines: (1) the author's inclusion and omission of traditional material; (2) the modifications of the material; (3) the arrangement of the material; and (4) contributions from the author's own theological intention.

LANGUAGE ANALYSIS

Another family of methodologies in the critical analysis of Scripture is concerned with language study. For several decades, Anglo-American philosophy has been preoccupied with the structure and logic of language. This movement has influenced Christian theology and has touched biblical scholarship particularly at the point of linguistics. The causation of language and its functions (expression, evocation, reference, etc.); the situations of the speaker and hearer; the genetic or social origins of language patterns; the social function; the creative, communitarian, or propagandist effects of language: these and the many other aspects of language origination and use are elements in the assessment of the way communication takes place. The particular choice of symbolic or expressive language used to produce conviction, shape identity, and lead to knowledge and experience of God is obviously of central concern to biblical scholars.

Quite naturally a number of these scholars turned to language philosophers and philologists for help in studying how language is used in Scripture and in the formulation of theology. Guidance has come from many sources, including the logical positivism of the Vienna School, the "language games" of Wittgenstein, and more recently from the structural linguistics of de Saussure and Levi-Strauss,[10] the "language acts" of John Austin, the sociolinguistics of Basil Bernstein, and the generative grammar of Noam Chomsky.

Another formative influence on theology and biblical studies has come from those philosophers who maintain that language is more than a means of communication with a structure and a series of finite laws governing its usage. Language, as viewed by thinkers such as Martin Heidegger and Paul Ricoeur, is a key—if not the master key—to unlocking the mystery of human existence.[11] In the study of Scripture this position implies that a text has not only a direct, primary, and literal sense but also an indirect, secondary, and figurative sense which can be apprehended only through the first. The hermeneutical task consists in discovering not only the obvious sense of the text but in deciphering the hidden meaning in the apparent meaning also, in unfolding those levels of meaning implied in the literal meaning.[12]

One particular linguistic methodology, structural analysis, deserves special mention because of the attention it is currently receiving in New Testament scholarship. This methodology is relatively new and takes a different tack than the more traditional historical-critical methodologies. Its focus is not so much on the historical as it is on how human beings assign meaning to the biblical text. In reaction to historicism and existentialism which have characterized historical-critical approaches, structuralism puts emphasis on the text itself. Form and redaction critics may be too obsessed with history, incorrectly identifying truth with facts and separating meaning from the message. This historical approach too easily locates the "message of the text in the sociohistorical context behind the text rather than in the text itself."[13] Bultmann, and those who follow him in the use of an existential hermeneutic, are guilty of separating the meaning from the message by making the meaning too anthropomorphic and subjective.

As a corrective, structuralists like Ferdinand de Saussure choose the text itself as the object of their reflection, rather than the author who composed it or the reader who reflects upon it. At the core of de Saussure's system of structural linguistics is the assumption that the human mind functions in certain ways called structures. It is not possible to fully understand the functioning of the human mind, but it is possible to discern its characteristics by an examination of its products. Literary words are especially appropriate for such a discernment because it is through language that the mind "expresses" itself. Thus the emphasis for the structuralist is on the relationship of the words to the text more than on the meaning of the words in the text intended by the original author. More emphasis is placed on *semiotics* (the study of the system of signs) than on *semantics* (the meaning of a sign). As applied to the New Testament the concern is to discover how the New Testament text creates a meaning effect, not how the New Testament came to be. It is perhaps too early to assess the place and value of this approach in biblical study, but its influence is certainly acknowledged by a wide cross-section of biblical scholars.

BIBLICAL THEOLOGY

One would think that the outgrowth of these various critical approaches to Scripture would be a body of information that would serve as a foundation for theology and proclamation. Textual, literary, historical, and linguistic analyses of the Bible are not ends in themselves but provide the raw materials out of which a viable theology may be constructed. The Bible may be viewed as a collection of language, literature, and history, but more importantly and profoundly the Bible is a book of faith. The work of biblical criticism should clear the way for the task of reflecting about God, the human condition, the life of faith, and the role of the church in the world. But the movement from biblical criticism to theology has been relatively slow, and more work needs to be done to construct a theology from a historical and philological (*sensus grammaticus*) understanding of the Bible.

The Bible for Theology and Church

We have argued that a preunderstanding based in faith and the use of a historical-critical approach are foundational for a hermeneutical approach that is to do justice to biblical revelation. Also needed is a conception of the Bible which preserves it as the Scripture of the church, as authoritative for theology and instructive for the common life of the Christian community. Four traditional concepts will be discussed in order to offer one way of achieving this goal. They are: canon, history, Word of God, and authority. These concepts individually and collectively are not problem-free, but they do constitute a frame of reference that has certain advantages for our study.

CANON

Basic to the preservation of the Bible as the Scripture of the church is the notion of canon. The books of the Old and New Testament constitute that body of literature that witnesses to the redemptive purpose of God for humanity. The value of this literature consists in its openness to God. What is recorded for us is the response of a people to God's revelation in their own peculiar time and situation. The people of God, whose story is told in the Bible, become the bearer of God's revelation. The story of the movement from the experience of God's guiding presence and redemptive action to its record in writing and acceptance by the believing community as Scripture (the canonical process) is long and complex and thus beyond our present scope. What is crucial to us here is to recognize that the story of Israel in the Old Testament is the story of one nation's destiny as the instrument of God; the many parts of it that appear to be merely chapters of secular history are necessary to the story because they reveal that God has claimed the whole of Israel's existence in service. But the story of God's dealings with Israel does not end with the crucifixion of Jesus; it continues throughout the New Testament as the church comes into being through God's continual unfolding of the divine will and way. The story of the original Israel and the story of the "new" Israel intermesh to form one story, and there is really but one family who claim Abraham, Moses, and David as "ancestors." The church is not founded on Christ and the teaching of the Apostles alone but also upon the witness of the Old Testament. These sixty-six books are "special" as canon because they uniquely tell the story of God's redemptive activity on behalf of humankind.

HISTORY

An appealing question might well be: why these people and why this history? The answer lies in the fact that the Scriptures bear a distinctive witness to actual events and revelatory experiences, and these events and experiences are unique. In chapter three we found that faith is intimately tied to actual historical events to which the Scriptures bear witness. The concept of "revelation in history" and its corollary, "revelatory event," have become problematic in recent years. The criticism is made that the term *history* has not only been used in an ambiguous way but that the concept is an abstraction foreign to all but a small portion of the Bible.[14] The criticism still does not invalidate the more general point which is being made here—namely, that God encountered this chosen people in time and space, and that this encounter, understood as event and experience, has a revelatory character.

WORD OF GOD

God is known not through universally attainable ideals but through a definite series of events at a particular time and place in history. The Bible is necessary if there is to be human access to these events. The Bible as a record of these events is not only an indispensable witness, it is an altogether fitting and appropriate witness because it is founded in a response of faith. The authors of Scripture do not presume to be objective recorders of inconsequential events, but rather, people who believe that God has spoken to them in these events. These events (and experiences) are construed to be the Word of God. The Bible, then, while not identical with the Word of God, is the appropriate access to the Word of God, and the Word cannot generally be heard except through the teaching and preaching of the Bible.

It is not altogether inappropriate to label the Bible "God's Word," though one should be careful not to treat the connection between Scripture and revelation statically. The Bible as a record of God's self-disclosure functions as the Word of God when it is faithfully proclaimed and received in faith. God by divine free act chooses to use the Scriptures to make the divine will and way known; hence the Bible becomes the Word of God as the Spirit of God uses it to create authentic faith and new life.

AUTHORITY

It follows that Scripture, as the writings which God uses to make the Word of God contemporaneous, should function with the authority in the church to shape individual and corporate life.[15] The Bible does indeed become the Word of God when it is heard in faith and begins to shape the identity of the hearer in distinctively Christian ways.[16] Through preaching, corporate worship, pastoral care, and Christian education in its many forms, the Scriptures are to be used to mold the lives of individual believers and congregations in a way which will empower them to fulfill the mission of the church. There are many patterns of Christian life, and no one pattern is a requirement for all, but certain attitudes and ethical practices are common to them all. The Scriptures become for the Christian community that body of literature that serves as a normative influence in creating these attitudes and actions. Theology is that particular point in the life of the Christian community when it pauses for self-assessment on its current life to see if that is true to its divine calling.[17] Theology is more than critical self-reflection, but certainly this function is a continual and never-ending part of it. Every generation of Christians must rewrite theology in order to insure that the church is fulfilling its mission in the world.

Interrelating the Four

This "package" of four concepts has several advantages as a way of conceiving the Bible for the Christian community. It preserves the unity of the Bible without forcing an artificial "Christian" interpretation onto the Old Testament. The Old Testament preserves its integrity but points to the New Testament as the fulfillment of God's redemptive activity on behalf of humankind.

Further, this package allows the Christian community to be informed, enriched, and nurtured by a wide diversity of literature which ranges across the varieties of human experience. History, poetry, story, psalm, epigram, and theological reflection all contribute to the spiritual enrichment of the church, as the church in its current situation has "conversation" with the ancient texts.[18] These concepts assert the Bible's central importance to the life of the church while avoiding the dangers of bibliolatry. Concepts such as infallibility and inerrancy may have value in certain contexts, but the risk in their use is that the case for the trustworthiness of the Scriptures may be overstated and therefore less convincing.

The four concepts presented above acknowledge the Bible's human and historical character, though not in a way that conflicts with its function as the mediator of revelation. They allow the Christian community to struggle honestly with the possibility of historical error in Scripture or to "argue" with a point of view of a particular biblical author without vitiating the Bible's revelatory character. This view also subordinates the Bible to the higher reality of God's self-disclosure, though continuing to maintain the place of Scripture as foundational for theology and church life. The Bible loses none of its authority, but neither does it replace the self-revelation of God in Jesus Christ as primary expression of the Word of God.

Finally, while it seems that no view of the Bible is free from controversy, this view does have the potential of bringing Christians of all confessions and denominations together in their common affirmation of the Bible's authority for theology and church life. It can accommodate a variety of viewpoints and provide a basis for ecumenical dialogue.

A Concluding Observation

An adequate methodology is essential in the interpretation of Scripture. It is impossible to render a fair and accurate interpretation of the text without understanding how to approach it. This is not to imply that there is only one approach. On the contrary, many approaches are necessary because of the many different types of literature which exist in the Bible. Thus coping with this variety is one of the distinctive challenges to the interpreter of Scripture as well.

SUGGESTED READING

Beardslee, William A. *Literary Criticism of the New Testament: Guides to Biblical Scholarship*. Philadelphia: Fortress, 1970.

Bultmann, Rudolf. *History of the Synoptic Tradition*. New York: Harper and Row, 1963.

Collins, Raymond F. *Introduction to the New Testament*. Garden City, NY: Doubleday, 1983.

Fee, Gordon D. *New Testament Exegesis: A Handbook for Students and Pastors*. Philadelphia: Westminster, 1983.

Finegan, Jack. *Encountering New Testament Manuscripts: A Working Introduction to Textual Criticism*. Grand Rapids: Eerdmans, 1974.

Koch, Klaus. *The Growth of the Biblical Tradition: The Form-Critical Method*. New York: Scribner's, 1969.

Krentz, Edgar. *The Historical Critical Method*. Philadelphia: Fortress, 1975.

McKnight, Edgar V. *What Is Form Criticism? Guides to Biblical Scholarship*. Philadelphia: Fortress, 1969.

Michelsen, A. Berkeley. *Interpreting the Bible*. Grand Rapids: Eerdmans, 1963.

Nineham, David E. *New Testament Interpretation in an Historical Age*. London: Athlone, 1976.

Patte, Daniel, and Aline Patte. *Structural Exegesis: From Theory to Practice*. Philadelphia: Fortress, 1978.

Perrin, Norman. *What Is Redaction Criticism?* Philadelphia: Fortress, 1969.

Peterson, Norman R. *Literary Criticism for New Testament Critics: Guides to Biblical Scholarship*. Philadelphia: Fortress, 1978.

Sanders, James. *A Guide to Canonical Criticism*. Philadelphia: Fortress, 1981.

Soulen, Richard N. *Handbook of Biblical Criticism*. Atlanta: John Knox, 1981.

5

Coping with Variety

The Diversity of the Biblical Literature

If general hermeneutics is concerned with the basic principles applicable to the interpretation of all literature, then special hermeneutics is concerned with establishing definitions and principles which guide in the interpretation of special literary forms and topical areas. History, poetry, prophecy, and theology differ from each in quite specific ways, and the interpreter must use "special" principles and methods appropriate to the particular character and style of the literature.

This requirement places an enormous demand on the interpreter who desires to use the entire Bible as a resource. Tremendous variations in language usage and literature types are present in the Bible. The busy pastor or the church school teacher called upon to preach and teach weekly from the Scriptures each needs a degree of familiarity with the concerns of special hermeneutics in order to render a fair and accurate interpretation of the text and passage. The purpose of this chapter is to provide some guidelines for interpreting the many different uses of language and literary forms which appear in the Bible.

Attempts at Unity: Typology, Allegory, and Analogy

One of the first tasks of the interpreter who wishes to work with the entire Bible is to find some order and pattern in the diverse elements of the whole. In chapter two various ways in which biblical scholars have understood the unity of the Bible were discussed, but certain categories which link together the various components of the Bible, and in particular those books within each respective Testament, were not emphasized. Any discussion of the unity of the Bible, especially after it has been asserted that Jesus Christ is the focal point of all Scripture, immediately raises the question of whether the hard-won victories in the name of a historical understanding of the Bible have all been in vain. There is the legitimate concern that any return to an interpretive approach may replace the literal meaning with allegorical and typological meaning. There have certainly been cases of such abuse, but it is also important to realize that some forms of typology and allegory *may* be validated in Scripture, and therefore these approaches should not be repudiated out of hand. On the other hand, neither should it be assumed that because there is a minimal use of typology and allegory in the Bible itself there is justification for their use in interpretation. It does suggest, however, that an investigation of such usages in Scripture is necessary if we are to understand what the biblical authors who utilize these approaches are trying to communicate.

Typology may be defined as the establishment of connections between persons, events, or objects in the Old Testament and persons, events, or objects in the New Testament. The reasoning is that there is a correspondence between the Old Testament and the New Testament, and that that which corresponds in the New Testament reshapes the meaning of the Old Testament. Behind the use of typology is the theological premise that it is God who controls all of history and who causes earlier individuals or events to embody characteristics which later are caused to reappear.

More generally, typological thinking arises out of the human effort to understand the world on the basis of analogy, symbol, and picture-image. When used in reference to the Bible, this understanding of typology has less to do with the specific events of saving history and more to do with understanding human existence in its relationship to salvation. The link between the Old and New Testaments is not found in this general system of religious ideas and values except in a very broad sense, as indeed it is in other religious literature. Its ultimate unity is found in saving history—that history set in motion by God which finds its denouement in the coming of Christ.

The most striking examples of this kind of typology in the Bible are found in comparing the events connected with Adam, Abraham, and Moses with those of Christ (Rom. 5:12–21; 1 Cor. 15:45–49; 2 Cor. 3:12–17; Heb. 3:1–6; et al.). The fact that typology is used in the Bible tends to impart validity to the method, but some care should be exercised in finding more "types" in the Old Testament than the Scriptures themselves warrant. There is in fact a renewed interest in this approach as a way of understanding the apparent connections between the Old and the New Testaments.[1]

Allegory is a method of interpreting Scripture that finds in the text a meaning different from its literal, surface, or historical meaning. Typology is historically oriented; allegory, though, rests more on the assumption that the literal sense conceals an eternal spiritual truth. Rabbinic Judaism makes free use of allegory, especially within the text of the Pentateuch, in order to reconcile inconsistencies and remove what appear to be absurdities in the text. Some writers of the New Testament have followed this practice (1 Cor. 9:8–12; Gal. 4:21–26; Heb. 7:2–10), and it was a common approach among early Christians up until the third century. This practice was revived again in the nineteenth century, based largely on an assumption rooted in German idealism that history is an organic whole. The gradual decline of this philosophical position, however, led interpreters of the Bible to look elsewhere for patterns of unity in Scripture. One direction in which they turned was toward spiritual interpretation—a view which moved away from the concrete saving event and pointed toward the universal "spiritual" truth.

The use of *analogy* as a principle of biblical interpretation is similar to typology in several respects. The logic is the same—people and events in the Old Testament correspond to people and events in the New Testament. Theologically speaking, the God who dealt with Israel throughout its history was the God of Jesus Christ, and the self-revelation of God's divinity in the personhood of Jesus Christ is the light which enables us to see more clearly the meaning of the divine Word and actions toward Israel. The advantage of the term *analogy* over typology is that it implies a less binding and exact correspondence. An example of such usage in Scripture is found in Ephesians 5 where Christ and his bride, the church, are said to be analogous to the relationship of husband and wife. The analogy in this case is straightforward and explained in the passage. Some theologians, however, may have tried to push this principle too far, as Barth, for instance, who claimed that the heaven and earth of Genesis 1:1 corresponds to the heavenly and earthly elements in Jesus Christ.

Language Usage

There is an immense variety of language used in the Bible.[2] Nearly every form of written communication is represented, and within this variety is a richness and vitality that makes the Bible one of the truly great pieces of literature in the world. Our discussion can only touch on this variety, and so we will select primarily those usages that tend to be the most difficult to understand.

One feature of the language in the Bible which makes interpretation more difficult is the use of figures of speech. A figure of speech is the representation of one idea or event in terms of another idea or event. Behind the use of figurative language is the assumption that there is a logical correspondence between the things compared which allows the analogy to be drawn. For example, when Jesus says, "I am the bread of life" (John 6:35), he is using a metaphor that compares how he sustains believers spiritually with how bread sustains them physically.

Figures of speech evolve out of the life and environment of the speaker or writer who uses them. Their primary purpose is to explain that which is unfamiliar to the reader or listener by a comparison with that which is familiar. Jesus is especially fond of figurative language and uses it extensively. He makes many points regarding the spiritual and ethical dimensions of life using comparisons to nature, to domestic and family life, to daily work, and to the religious customs of his listeners. For Jesus, imagery is an extremely effective way to communicate; it is the language which enables human beings to understand themselves and their relationship with God.

COMPARISON

The most common type of figurative language is the one-for-one comparison. It may take the form of *simile,* as when two unlike things are compared, the comparison typically made explicit by the use of *like* or *as*. Again, Jesus provides us with an abundance of examples, as in his description of the end times: "For as the lightning comes from the east and shines as far as the west, so will be the coming of the Son of man" (Matt. 24:27).

Metaphor also compares the object it ordinarily designates to an object it may designate only by implicit connection or analogy. Metaphors are common to Jesus but are found also in the Old Testament. Most often it is God who is described metaphorically, as when the divine power and victory are spoken of by reference to a hand or an arm: "You shall remember that you were a servant in the land of Egypt, and the LORD your God brought you out thence with a mighty hand and an outstretched arm" (Deut. 5:15).

ASSOCIATION

Another common figure of speech is *metonymy,* which involves the usage of one word or a phrase for another, the two being associated together and suggestive of each other. Paul, for example, uses the terms *circumcised* and *uncircumcised* to represent Jew and Gentile (Rom. 3:30).

Similar is *synecdoche* in which a part is used for a whole or a whole for a part. In Micah 4:3 we read: "And they shall beat their swords into plowshares, and their spears into pruning hooks." Here two weapons, swords and spears, represent the total disarmament of a nation.

Personification is another form of the associative use of language. It occurs when an inanimate object or abstraction takes on the qualities of a human personality. Jesus, for example, gives days the capacity to feel anxiety: "Therefore do not be anxious about tomorrow, for tomorrow will be anxious for itself. Let the day's own trouble be sufficient for the day" (Matt. 6:34).

SUGGESTION

On occasion a biblical author will not fully express the thought of a sentence or paragraph, allowing the reader to supply the words or thoughts needed to make the unit complete. This type of language is usually called *ellipsis* and is occasionally found in the writings of

Paul. In 1 Corinthians 6:12 Paul writes: "'All things are lawful for me,' but not all things are helpful. 'All things are lawful for me,' but I will not be enslaved by anything." Several phrases need to be supplied in order to make this verse explicit and complete.

A further use of suggestion, called *aposiopesis,* occurs when part of a sentence is suppressed. This technique is used by the author to achieve a calculated effect on the reader, usually suggesting serious consequences. When Jesus was questioned by the religious leaders regarding the basis of his authority for teaching, Jesus replies with a counterquestion: "Was the baptism of John from heaven or from men? Answer me." The religious leaders debated, and then replied: "If we say, 'From heaven,' he will say, 'Why then did you not believe him?' But shall we say, 'From men'?" (Mark 11:30–32). The implication of the final statement "From men?" is that if they so answered, they would have to deal with the anger of the people, who believed John to be a genuine prophet—a point which Mark adds in his account.

DISTORTION

From time to time, a biblical author will slightly distort the straightforward expression of a thought in order to bring out a more subtle shade of meaning. A *euphemism* is the substitution of an inoffensive term for one considered to be offensive. For example, the phrase "come near" may refer to a sexual approach (Gen. 20:4, KJV), but to use this phrase rather than a more explicit one gives the sentence a slightly different overtone.

Hyperbole is another example of distortion. It involves a conscious use of exaggeration in order to make an impact on the reader or listener. Moses, on reporting what the spies saw across the Jordan, says: "The people are greater and taller than we; the cities are great and fortified up to heaven" (Deut. 1:28).

When a writer or speaker uses words to mean the opposite of what the language declares, this is often a case of *irony.* This figure of speech is also commonly used in the Bible. Jesus, in denouncing the scribes and Pharisees, says to them: "For you build the tombs of the prophets and adorn the monuments of the righteous" (Matt. 23:29).

His intent, of course, is to show their hypocrisy by extolling what some might take to be acts of virtue.

OBFUSCATION

There are sections of the Bible in which the meaning remains unclear and indistinct, at times intentionally so by the author, and at other times because the original intent of the author is lost behind the curtain of centuries, culture, and language. The passages whose meaning is lost remain forever a challenge, but those in which the author intended obfuscation can generally be deciphered.

The use of *riddle* is not uncommon, and good examples can be found throughout the book of Revelation (see, e.g., Rev. 13:18). The *fable*, a fictitious story with a moral or religious lesson, is also utilized by biblical authors. Ezekiel 17 is a good example. There are a number of places in the Bible also where *enigma* occurs and requires of the reader or listener careful thought in order to discover the meaning. The Gospels record many sayings of Jesus which have an enigmatic quality, as, for example, when Jesus says, "But many that will be first will be last, and the last first" (Matt. 19:30).

EXTENSION

It is common in the Bible to find figures of speech expanded beyond a phrase or sentence into a full story, as in the case of a parable or an allegory. The *parable* is an extended simile which takes the form of a simple story. Like the fable it too almost invariably illustrates a moral or religious lesson. The parable was used extensively by Jesus as a means of communicating his central message of the kingdom of God. Jesus uses parable in a way which puts a special burden on the hearer or reader to respond to God's reign and demands. The imagery and content of Jesus' parables come from the surroundings and everyday life of the hearers, insuring that the listener will be able to "hear" the message being communicated. One basic principle to keep in mind when interpreting parables is to attempt to isolate the main point, rather than attempting to read meaning into every detail.

Allegory is essentially an extended metaphor in which each part carries an ethical or spiritual meaning. In the allegory of the good shepherd (John 10:11–16) Jesus assigns meaning to the door, the shepherd, the sheep, and the flock. The same is true for the allegory of the vine and the branches (John 15:1–8). Allegory used in a didactic approach such as these should not be confused with allegorical interpretation, a mode of interpretation which finds "hidden" meaning in the usual or customary sense conveyed by words or expressions.

SIGNIFICATION

A *sign* or *symbol* uses an object to represent something else, either by association, resemblance, or convention. It is commonly used by biblical authors to convey some lesson or truth, and fortunately the lesson or truth to be conveyed is often revealed by the author. Whenever the meaning has not been made clear, later generations of readers often have difficulty discerning the appropriate meaning as, for example, in the book of Revelation. One common symbol used in both the Old and New Testaments is blood, which is customarily associated with atonement (e.g., Lev. 17:11; Heb. 9:22). Other signs and symbols used in the Bible are certain numbers, names, colors, metals, jewels, and even certain events. One of the most important uses of symbol in the New Testament is in the sacraments (ordinances). The wine, the bread, the water, etc. all point beyond themselves to a profound spiritual truth.

Variety of Genre

In addition to the tremendous diversity of language usage, the Bible is also distinguished by containing several different types of literature. Each type of literature (genre) has its own distinctive character and requires that appropriate principles and approaches be employed by the interpreter. Books have been written about each type of literature; here we shall do no more than try to survey these types.

LAW

The first five books of the Old Testament, the Pentateuch, are often referred to as "the law," although they contain more than legal codes. The essence of the law in the Old Testament is the Ten Commandments (Exod. 20:3–17; Deut. 5:6–21), and these ten principles constitute the foundation of the elaborate system of legislation which developed in the history of the Hebrew people. The oldest legal code in the Hebrew system of law is the Covenant code (Exod. 20:22—23:33) which may have been developed as early as a century or two after Moses.

Both the written and the oral law were regarded by the Hebrews as inspired by God and not to be altered. But even they admitted that there was a gradual development of the law, as the scholars of the law sought to make it applicable to particular circumstances. Three fundamental principles guided the Hebrew people in the application of the law to the situations in which they found themselves: (1) life was sacred, of more value, even, than the law itself; (2) parents deserved respect and carried authority as a way of preserving the stability of family life; (3) there should be no other god (loyalty) before God, an attitude of supreme importance.

In the New Testament the concept of law occurs frequently, although it is conceived differently than in the Old Testament. The attitude of Jesus toward the Old Testament law was one of respect, although he had little patience with the excessive legalism it seemed to foster and so was willing to challenge traditional interpretations of the law. Paul prior to his conversion to Christian faith was an ardent student and loyal follower of Jewish law. In time he came to view the law as a temporary guardian necessary to reveal human sinfulness, to be replaced in humankind's relation to God, however, by the life of faith.

At least three basic hermeneutical principles should guide the interpreter in the study of those sections of the Bible that deal with the law:

1. Much of the specific content of the legal codes found in the Old Testament has little bearing on the life of the modern Christian, but the intent of the law to insure genuine piety and justice has enormous relevance for modern Christianity and the world.

2. The core of the law represented in the Ten Commandments and epitomized by Jesus (Matt. 22:36–40) has as much importance to the Christian today as it did when it was first stated.[3]

3. For the Christian, the Old Testament legal code is no longer

binding as a way of achieving God's favor. As Paul teaches with such clarity, through justification by faith there is freedom from the old restrictions (Rom. 5:1ff.; Gal. 3—5).

HISTORY

Much of the Bible is in the form of history. Twelve books in the Old Testament and five in the New[4] have a distinctly historical character. It is in and through the history of a given people that the specific religious message of the Bible unfolds. The revelation of God takes place in history, and God accomplishes the divine purpose and makes the divine will known in the lives and events of people and nations.

Four distinct historical periods may be distinguished in the Bible. First, there is the account of the creation of the universe and all which it contains, including the human race. The purpose of this account is to show God as Creator and Lord and to introduce human history, though some caution should be exercised in using the term *history* in reference to the creation accounts (Gen. 1:1—2:3).

Second, there is a brief account of early human history showing God's relation to humankind, laying the foundation for the selection of a chosen people (Gen. 2:4—11:26). These events fall almost entirely into a "prehistoric" period and are divided into two sections by the flood. Again, one should use the term *history* in reference to the description in Genesis somewhat selectively and with careful definition.

The third major unit of history in the Bible is the story of the chosen people. It begins with an independent tribe in Canaan under the leadership of Abraham, Isaac, and Jacob, proceeds to a description of the twelve tribes and the bondage in Egypt, and concludes with the account of the nation constituted at Sinai as it progresses through several stages.

The final segment of history recorded in the Bible is the establishment of the Christian church. There is the account of Jesus in the Gospels and of the church's expansion throughout the Roman world in Acts and in other parts of the New Testament. As the interpreter approaches the historical sections of the Bible, the following guidelines should be kept in mind:

1. The ancient biblical authors were not historians in the modern sense. Their purpose was primarily to impart a religious message as it was contained in the events of a people, not to scientifically check the accuracy of every source. It is this religious message that continues to speak to the people of God today.

2. The historical events are themselves important insofar as they "carry" the revelation of God. Although it is not possible (or necessary) to verify or check every detail of every event, it is nevertheless important to stress the centrality of historical event as the carrier of revelation. God is made known in the particulars of time and place.

3. The interpreter need not fear the use of the term *myth*[5] in reference to certain of the events which are described in the Bible. Myth is characterized by the fact that it sees the empirical world and its happenings, and above all, human beings, in the light of a reality which constitutes them, makes them a unity, and at the same time transcends them. In the Bible, this reality is God. The function of myth is the explanation of the origin of principles which guide all subsequent related events. Myth, then, should not be regarded as fiction or fantasy, but as a deeper truth about the meaning and purpose which stand behind it all. In those sections of Scripture dealing with creation and prehistoric times, myth is indeed a legitimate classification if it is understood as an expression of a profound theological truth.

POETRY

Job, Psalms, Proverbs, Ecclesiastes, and the Song of Solomon are usually classified as the poetic books of the Bible, although there are sections in them that are not poetry, and there are other books elsewhere in the Bible where poetry does occur. Poetry is one of the earliest forms through which the literary pulse of a people begins to express itself. The poetry of the Bible is rhythmic and regular in form; it may be compared to the motions of a dancer, which it occasionally accompanied in ancient times (Exod. 15:20–21). This poetry grows out of the emotions of the people; it was how individual or national joy or sorrow or deep concern was expressed. The song of Moses and Miriam (Exod. 15:1–21), commemorating the overthrow of Pharaoh at sea, is archetypal. It is one of the earliest expressions of Hebrew poetry known.

Ancient Hebrew poetry does not rhyme, nor is its meter always regular. The essential formal characteristic is parallelism—i.e., the thought or sentiment of one line is echoed in the next. This parallelism takes many forms: at times, the echo is synonymous with the first line (Ps. 22:20); at times, a logical progression of thought (Prov. 26:4); often it is climactic (Ps. 121:3–4); and occasionally antithetic (Matt. 8:20), or comparative (Ps. 42:1). The most common form of poetry in the Bible is the lyric, which usually appears as triumphal odes celebrating victories or as expressions of pain, distress, or praise.

The interpreter of biblical poetry should keep in mind the following principles:

1. As far as possible, discover the historical setting out of which the poetry emerges. The historical circumstances are often the necessary clue to understanding the author's intent.

2. Carefully study the language of the poetry for images and figures of speech. It is through the imagery that the subtle meaning of the poem is conveyed.

3. Observe the basic convictions of the poet about the being of God or the nature of the human condition. The poetry of the Bible speaks poignantly to these subjects.

PROPHECY

Seventeen books in the Old Testament are traditionally classified as prophetic, five (Isaiah, Jeremiah, Lamentations, Ezekiel, and Daniel) are referred to as major prophets, and twelve (Hosea, Joel, Amos, Obadiah, Jonah, Micah, Nahum, Habakkuk, Zephaniah, Haggai, Zechariah, and Malachi) as minor prophets. Prophecy occurs elsewhere in the Bible, and there are passages in these seventeen books which are not technically prophecy. Much of Daniel, for example, might be better classified as apocalyptic.

The prophet is a divinely inspired preacher who speaks for God and declares God's will to the people. The message of the prophet does not concern itself primarily with the foretelling of future events in the sense of prediction. It deals rather with forth-telling or proclaiming the will of God in a specific setting in the life of an individual or nation. Elijah, for example, speaks directly to King Ahab (1 Kings 18) regarding his complicity in causing Israel's problems.

The Hebrew prophets felt themselves to be spiritual leaders authorized by God to warn their contemporaries of the consequences of evil and to point the way to righteousness and true religious faith. The five hundred years of the prophetic movement initiated by Amos (ca. 750 B.C.) was at the heart of Israel's spiritual greatness. Bold, even in the presence of danger and power, they preached the holiness of God, the perils of injustice, and the necessity of patriotic loyalty.

There has been a wide range of hermeneutical approaches used in the interpretation of prophecy in the Bible, ranging from those who would almost totally stress the predictive aspect to those who would understand the prophetic message only in reference to the historical context in which it was expressed by the prophet. It is not possible here to assess the respective strengths and weaknesses of the various approaches, but one should be careful not to overemphasize the predictive element. The following principles should guide the interpreter in the explication of the prophetic books of the Bible:

1. The prophetic passage should be carefully studied in terms of its historical and cultural setting. To know the historical background of the prophet and the specific circumstances to which the prophetic message is addressed will assure the interpreter of discerning the primary intent of the passage.

2. If the passage is predictive in tone, the interpreter should observe whether any conditions are attached, and whether it is "fulfilled" or "unfulfilled." If the prophecy has been fulfilled, it is important to understand all the historical circumstances of the fulfillment. If unfulfilled, then the interpreter might well ask why or whether the prophet's message is indeed pointing to a time yet in the future.

3. Avoid imposing onto the text, especially those texts that are filled with imagery and symbol, meaning which would not have been entirely clear to the original author. There are exceptions to this rule of thumb, but its general application will reduce the temptation to use the Scriptures as a sort of crystal ball.

DOCTRINE

The writing attributed to the Apostle Paul in the New Testament, as well as several other epistles, including Hebrews, James, 1 and 2 Peter, 1, 2, and 3 John, and Jude, have been traditionally classified as doctrinal. The Greek noun *didaskalia,* often translated as doctrine, is derived from a verb whose active meaning is to teach or instruct; thus in the passive it means that which is taught. The teaching of "sound" doctrine (1 Tim. 1:8–11; 2 Tim. 4:1–4; Titus 1:9; 2:1) is the fundamental motif of this literature. It is intended to guide the reader in all aspects of Christian faith including beliefs and practice. Some of the material is directed to specific circumstances in a particular church setting (e.g., 1 Cor. 8 treats food offered to idols), but the larger portion of the material has a universal character about it. Romans, for example, is Paul's statement about the essence of Christian faith and practice and except for a few minor details could have been distributed to any of the churches with which Paul was in contact.

The interpreter must take into account a number of factors in approaching these twenty-one books and the many other passages of Scripture that are doctrinal in character.

1. The interpreter should once again be especially conscious about imposing a modern point of view onto the text. It is altogether too easy to make a doctrinal passage fit a preconceived theological framework. There are equal risks in having no framework in which to understand the text, but the essential point for the interpreter is to be aware of how a particular ideological construct provides a context for understanding a passage.

2. As before, the interpreter should be sensitive to the uses of language and conscientious about studying the historical and cultural setting of the author and destination of the literature.

3. Special attention needs to be given to a precise formulation of exactly what the passage is teaching. This can only be done by thorough historical study and careful exegesis, a practice that will help the interpreter to avoid finding a "proof text" for a personal belief or cultural folk wisdom.

APOCALYPTIC

Only two books of the Bible, Revelation and Daniel, may be classified as apocalyptic, although there are passages in other books of the Bible which have the features of apocalyptic literature. This genre is characterized by a general despair over present conditions, a warning about coming judgment, and a conviction that ultimately God will dramatically intervene and vindicate the divine, righteous will. This message is consistently written with extensive use of figurative language. Daniel, the only book in the Old Testament with apocalyptic elements, fits this pattern as much or more so than it does the prophetic. Revelation is described by its author as a communication about "what must soon take place." As in Daniel, the readers of this book are experiencing persecution and are unsure of how their experiences fit into God's plan and purpose for them.

John, as the author is called, writes to give them comfort and guidance, using symbolism characteristic of apocalyptic literature. Occasionally, John appears to be deliberately cryptic in order to avoid danger from the persecutors, but generally the expressed desire is to be understood and a form of communication with which first century readers were familiar is used. Unfortunately, though, the key to the symbolism employed has been partially lost, and thus those who claim to have a full understanding of what John is saying may have more enthusiasm than knowledge. Still, to understand the essential message of Revelation, one must discover the author's intent for the book and the message which is being communicated to its readers. The author believed that God was about to intervene in history, that there would be a series of events which would soon take place and would bring the present order to an end, ushering in a new age. Revelation is written to prepare its readers for these events and calls on them to be people of faith and hope. Its message takes the form of seven visions representing these coming events.

Interpretations of Revelation are numerous and fall into four general classifications. (1) The *contemporary-historical interpretation* regards the work as a description of what was taking place when the book was written. (2) The *futurist interpretation* sees in the book predictions of events yet to be fulfilled. (3) The *historical-prophetic interpretation* views the book as a portrayal of events of Christian history and of the world from the first century to the end of time. (4) The *spiritual-symbolic interpretation* regards the visions as descriptions of religious principles which are true for Christians in any age. Whatever method of interpretation is employed, it is essential that the interpreter be conscious of the following considerations:

1. The book can only be understood by a careful study of the author's intention and the historical circumstances of the readers.

2. Much of the symbolism (code language) of the book is from the Old Testament, and a referencing of symbol with the Old Testament can often shed light on the meaning of the symbol.

3. The eschatological element cannot be totally minimized without doing an injustice to the straightforward meaning of the texts (see 1:1, 19; 20:5–10; 22:20).

4. A humble I-don't-know-for-sure about some of the details of the book is not inappropriate, even for the best trained biblical scholar.

Interpreting Scripture

What general principles of hermeneutics emerge from this brief survey of language usage and types of literature which appear in the Bible? At the risk of oversimplification, let me here suggest ten.

1. The Bible should be interpreted in view of the fact that human language cannot "contain" its primary subject, God. The language of the Bible, indeed all language, is limited by the capacity of the human mind and by the historical era and culture in which it is spoken. The truth of God must be accommodated to these limitations, which is to say the Bible contains the truth of God in human thought forms. There is, then, of necessity an anthropomorphic character to the language of the Bible. The Bible speaks of God in symbol and imagery, pointing to a truth which transcends the language used, which would be true no matter what the language used. The language used in speaking of God, being analogical in character, allows us to understand God in terms with which we can identify.

2. The interpreter of the Bible should keep in mind that there is a

progression throughout the Old Testament which reaches its climax in the New Testament. The historical progression is obvious, but more importantly there is the promise or covenant of the Old Testament which finds its fulfillment in the New. A hermeneutical approach which finds typological or Christological correspondence on every page of the Old Testament distorts the meaning of the Old Testament. But to affirm that the Old Testament can and should be understood in light of the New Testament is to acknowledge that God has been at work with the faithful across the centuries.

3. The Bible should be interpreted on a sound grammatical and historical basis. The best tools of language study and all of the resources of modern day historiography should be employed. As far as possible, all interpretations should be based on a study of the original languages.

4. The interpreter should consciously attempt to "stand under" the passage and discover its meaning rather than impose his or her own preunderstanding onto it. This is not to imply that the interpreter can or ever should be an entirely "empty vessel," but it means that the passage must be allowed to stand on its own and speak for itself.

5. Generally, the interpreter should give preference to the straightforward and obvious meaning of the passage. To find hidden meaning and symbolic language where none is intended is to run the risk of distorting the author's original intention. Along the same line, the interpreter should attempt to discover the one meaning intended by the author and avoid suggesting more than one meaning unless the text itself suggests it.

6. The interpreter should allow obscure passages to give way to clear passages. If there is some unity of purpose and theme in the Bible as we have maintained, then those passages which are clear can shed light on those passages where the meaning is not apparent. The classical principle of the analogy of faith which states that there is perfect harmony in the Bible on the fundamental issues of faith and practice may partially violate a historical understanding of the Bible, but its value is to be found in the fact that it suggests there is commonality of theme in the various books of the Bible, and that one passage can assist the interpreter in understanding another passage. One additional point in reference to obscure passages: it is

certainly in order for the interpreter to admit ignorance about the meaning.

7. On the basis of the insight contained in the analogy of faith, the interpreter should allow systematic passages to interpret incidental passages. In the writings of Paul, for example, the system of thought which he develops in Romans and Galatians can be helpful in interpreting incidental references in his other letters.

8. On the same premise, the interpreter should understand local customs and events in light of universal principles. Jesus masterfully teaches his disciples about love and humility in washing their feet, but the custom would have little relevance in a culture that does not use sandals. A precise line cannot always be drawn between the local and universal, but the principle is still valid and can be useful to the interpreter.

9. Again, following the insight contained in the analogy of faith, the interpreter should allow didactic passages to aid in the interpretation of symbolic passages. The teachings of Jesus in the Olivet discourse and a large part of the book of Revelation can be illuminated by other passages of Scripture in which similar subjects are discussed. Care should be taken not to force an artificial unity onto the Bible, but where there is clearly an overlap, especially common authorship, then the didactic passages can legitimately give assistance in understanding the symbolic passages.

10. Finally, the interpreter who comes to the Bible with faith in the God about whom it speaks has the special empathy and capacity to understand its life-giving message. The preunderstanding of faith allows the interpreter to "hear" and apprehend rather than merely to master the technical details of language and history.

These "Ten Commandments," with all their obvious limitations, can assist the interpreter to understand the message of the Bible and communicate it to those who long to hear it.

SUGGESTED READING

Blackman, E. C. *Biblical Interpretation*. Philadelphia: Westminster, 1957.

Briggs, R. C. *Interpreting the Gospels*. Nashville: Abingdon, 1969.

———. *Interpreting the New Testament Today*. Nashville: Abingdon, 1973.

Caird, G. G. *The Language and Imagery of the Bible*. Philadelphia: Westminster, 1980.
Efird, James M. *How to Interpret the Bible*. Atlanta: John Knox, 1984.
Marshall, I. Howard. *New Testament Interpretation: Essays on Principles and Methods*. Grand Rapids: Eerdmans, 1977.
Ramm, Bernard. *Protestant Biblical Interpretation*. Boston: W. A. Wilde, 1950.
Smart, James D. *The Interpretation of Scripture*. Philadelphia: Westminster, 1961.
Sproul, R. C. *Knowing Scripture*. Downers Grove, IL: InterVarsity, 1977.
Stacey, David. *Interpreting the Bible*. New York: Seabury, 1979.
Terry, Milton S. *Biblical Hermeneutics*. Grand Rapids: Zondervan, 1974.
von Hoffman, J. C. K. *Interpreting the Bible*. Minneapolis: Augsburg, 1959.
Westermann, Claus. *Essays on Old Testament Hermeneutics*. Atlanta: John Knox, 1960.

6

Using the Bible

In Theology

Historically, Christian theologians have generally acknowledged a crucial link between theology and Scripture. A few, both ancient and modern, have seen fit to question the primacy of this connection, but this questioning has consistently come from a small minority. The virtually universal consensus among theologians, however, regardless of ecclesiastical heritage, era of history, or theological orientation, is that theology is to be done in some sense "in accord with Scripture."

Assuming this, it seems to follow that the theologian's responsibility involves molding the many diverse elements of the Bible into a coherent pattern and drawing out the implications of biblical teaching for the believing community in a given generation. More specifically, Christian theology may be defined as the science of the faith which is rooted in the biblical revelation. It is a rational and critical reflection, explanation, and explication of divine revelation and has as its purpose the guidance of the church.

The term *theology* has been and continues to be used in other ways. For example, it is occasionally associated with the general study of religion, or at times used to describe a branch of philosophy which deals with ultimate questions. Within the theological seminary it is often defined more narrowly as a specific discipline among many other disciplines which are engaged in reflecting upon the meaning of the Christian faith. The generic sense of the term, though, involves the study of God's self-communication, understanding that the domain of theology covers all the implications of this self-disclosure.

One of the most difficult tasks for the theologian, even if this inseparable link is assumed, is to clarify the nature of the Bible's authority for theology. Theologians have not always agreed on the meaning of the concept of the authority of Scripture for theology. They have in fact used the Bible in their theological work in quite different ways.[1] But in general the concept has been taken to mean that theological proposals are under the authority of Scripture insofar as Scripture informs them and controls their content. The Bible functions to establish the agenda for theology and to suggest the direction for the expansion and development of the subjects on the agenda.

Scripture may also be said to be *normative* for theology because it prescribes its content, pattern, and standard. The words *authoritative* and *normative* have similar but slightly different connotations. *Authoritative* emphasizes more the aspect of control whereas *normative* suggests more the pattern. Both words are used regularly and are helpful in clarifying the relationship between the Bible and theology.

Justification for the work of theology is to be found in the Bible itself. The Bible is filled with reflections about the meaning of divine revelation. Jesus taught regularly from the context of the Old Testament and made teaching one of the central features of his ministry. People were astonished at his teaching (Matt. 7:28), and he claimed that the substance of his teaching was from God (John 7:16). Paul made reference to doctrine (standard of teaching) and urged an obedience to it which comes from the heart (Rom. 6:17). Christians are cautioned against being "tossed to and fro and carried about with every wind of doctrine" (Eph. 4:14), and Timothy is urged to be careful to preserve sound doctrine throughout the two epistles which carry his name. The Bible itself, then, gives a mandate to provide sound teaching (doctrine or theology), which grows out of reflection on God's self-disclosure, in order to guide the Christian community.

In what ways does the theologian provide "sound doctrine" which serves to guide the church? There are at least three essential tasks of theology insofar as it is used by and for the church. The first and most obvious is to provide a *way of thinking about faith*. Even the simplest Christian faith has a doctrinal element. A person cannot become fully Christian without knowing something about God, God's forgiveness, the person and work of Jesus, and the presence of the Holy Spirit. To understand the Bible's teaching on these matters and to make them personal is a vital part of what it means to be a Christian. The theologian has responsibility to provide the categories and systems that give coherence to the cognitive content of faith. Traditionally, this function has been called catechetical instruction.

A second responsibility of the theologian, one which has provided much of the motivation for theology from the beginning, is to *guard against heresy*—those teachings which are contrary to biblical faith. Substitute "gospels" and distortions of all kinds were presented to the early church and have been present ever since. Often these distortions have their own inherent logic and persuasion and can subtly cause the church to exchange its divine treasure for "yellow gold." Here the argument is not for a single theological position or a suggestion for any form of censorship or control. Theological exploration should be encouraged, and the various theological traditions of the church can and should inform and enrich one another. But there is an ongoing necessity of distinguishing between truth and error, between that which brings new life and that which is harmful and destructive to the Christian community.

A third task of theology is to *provide direction for the church's on-going life* in order to insure that the church remains faithful to its biblically defined mission in the world. The theologian has a responsibility to assist the church to be reflective about its corporate life and to guide the church in an assessment of whether it is meeting its obligation to be an instrument of God in the world. The theologian uses Scripture in this critical assessment to judge whether the church is enabling individuals and groups to be all that God intends them to be.

These three specific tasks and their many variations constitute the primary responsibility of the Christian theologian. But how the theologian fulfills this responsibility needs further amplification. A fundamental challenge for the theologian is to discover how the Bible and theology are related, and a number of categories and metaphors have been used in attempts to describe the relationship. One category commonly used is *extension,* implying that theology is an expansion of the grammatical-historical understanding of a text or passage. This concept suggests that the theologian's responsibility, once the primary meaning of the biblical passage has been ascertained, is to restate it in an enlarged form in a way which will draw out its significance for the life of the church and the community it serves. It is assumed in this concept that there is an unbroken connection between the Bible and what the theologian says regarding the text or passage. Also, the concept does not identify specific directions or limitations for the enlargement, although the parameters for enlargement can be determined apart from the application of the concept itself.

Another metaphor commonly used is that of *translation*. This notion begins with the assumption that the Bible and modern Christians speak different languages. The theologian's task is to translate the language of the Bible (prescientific, mythological, Hebraic, etc.) into contemporary idiom which is understandable and applicable today. Defined in this way, theology is a never ending task, that of restating the message of the Bible in thought forms and language which make it relevant and life-giving to the believing community. Theology enables the biblical message to leap over language and cultural barriers and speak a powerful and transforming word in a new cultural setting. The metaphor assumes a continuity of meaning between theological proposal and Scripture. The metaphor, though, does seem to assume that there is *one* "message" of the Bible which can be translated into the *one* current idiom, an assumption that is difficult to defend in our diverse contemporary world.

A third term used in describing the connection between the Bible and theology is *synopsis*. In this view the theologian has the responsibility of collecting and summarizing all that the Bible says on any given subject. Theology is to provide a synoptic view of the Bible's teaching about a variety of subjects, including bibliology (the doctrine of the Scriptures), theology (the doctrine of God), Christology (the doctrine of Jesus Christ), pneumatology (the doctrine of the Holy Spirit), anthropology (the doctrine of humanity), hamartiology (the doctrine of sin), soteriology (the doctrine of salvation), ecclesiology (the doctrine of the church), and eschatology (the doctrine of last things). A clear limitation of this category is that there is no real acknowledgment of the role of the theologian's preunderstanding in the selection and arrangement of the material in the development of each subject.

A final category often used to connect the Bible and theology is *image*. If theology is understood as the task of imaginatively reproducing the content of the Bible in a way which is most helpful to the church, the theologian, so conceived, has some similarity to an artist in the attempt to creatively capture the "spirit" of the subject. The theologian imaginatively construes the Bible in a way which expresses how God is present among believers. The risk in this view is that there are no clearly stated limits assigned to the theologian's imagination, thus allowing for the possibility that the locus of theology becomes the imagination of the theologians rather than the Bible.

A number of other categories and metaphors have been proposed to describe the linkage between theology and the Bible. These four, however, have been most commonly used; and taken together with their respective strengths they constitute a good description of the relationship between the Bible and theology.

Theologians are generally an independent lot, known in recent times more and more for speaking and writing in ways governed only by their own conscience. This is how it should be, for the church needs its most sensitive and creative minds at work in a supportive environment producing theological literature to guide and instruct the church. Yet one does not do the work of theology in a vacuum, but in reference to principles and traditions which have served the discipline for centuries. Given the present conditions that exist in the discipline of theology and in the life of the church, the following principles seem especially important at this time.

1. *The theologian should operate under the normative control of the Bible*. This may seem an unnecessary and a far too obvious point to make, but increasingly there have been those who would argue that theology need not be practiced in reference to the Bible. There should be no quarrel with those who explore philosophical and theological questions outside of a biblical frame of reference, especially as it is done as a part of the academic study of religion. The work may be of great interest and value, but it is putatively not done primarily to enable the church to accomplish its mission. The church

is a community which finds its purpose and identity in reference to the Bible, and therefore it follows that the theologian who serves the church does theology in dialogue with the Bible.

2. *The theologian needs to be governed by the general principles of hermeneutics, and base theology on a grammatical-historical understanding of the Bible.* In the development of a system or in the desire to cogently express a point of view, far too often do theologians violate sound hermeneutical maxims. Even Karl Barth, whose *Church Dogmatics* is one of the most impressive attempts in our century to produce a theology rooted in the biblical revelation, occasionally is quite indifferent to and even aloof from the work of biblical scholarship. For him, revelation is a sheer miracle and shines by its own light, and biblical research may even be irrelevant to it. Barth's point should be grasped, but it should not carry the day. A theology which is grounded in the biblical revelation and undergirded by the finest biblical scholarship will best serve the church in the long run.

3. *The theologian should be explicit about presuppositions regarding the nature of the Bible.* It is not necessary for all theologians to view the Bible in the same way. Indeed, the fact that the Bible has been understood differently has created a theological dialogue of diversity which enriches the church. But what is crucial is that the theologian write theology consistent with his or her presuppositions about the Bible. Only by so doing will the theologian be doing theology under the aegis of Scripture.

In what sense is the Bible inspired? In what way is it or does it contain revelation? How is it authoritative for theology and church life? How does it function as a normative guide to the theologian in doing the work of theology? How far does the theologian go with the premises and work of the historical criticism of the Bible? The result of the theologian's work will be substantially influenced by the kind of answers given to these and other questions about the nature of the Bible.

The theology of Rudolf Bultmann serves us as a good example here. His theology is distinctly tied to his understanding of the Bible. He holds that the Bible is best understood and made relevant to modern people when its prescientific categories are demythologized.

Then new categories, more in line with the way modern people think, can be substituted. He suggests the existentialism of Martin Heidegger as a basic frame of reference for encasing the message in the Bible, allowing it to speak with poignancy to moderns. Bultmann has great freedom to interpret the Bible this way because of the presuppositions he holds about the Bible, e.g., that it has a prescientific frame of reference, and that it is the Bible's message and not its inspired words that modern people need to hear.

4. *The theologian must be clear about the theological method that is employed.* Again, no one theological method should be singled out as the only way to approach the practice of theology. But Scripture and theological method are intimately connected, and the quality of the theological work hinges on the consistency with which the two are joined.

By theological method we mean the orderly and systematic procedure which the theologian employs in the writing of theology. It contains assumptions about epistemology and more particularly about how the Scriptures contain or point to the truth of God. It also serves as an organizational bridge between Scripture and the writing of theology. For example, the approach may be deductive, beginning with a universal biblical proposition from which all other theological proposals flow, or it may be inductive, beginning with the data of Scripture and the human condition. It may even start with an orientation to the human situation or with reflection on the nature of God. Each approach defines a starting point and a direction in which the theologian is to proceed.

An attempt should also be made to correlate the questions being raised by modern people as a result of living in a complex and confusing world with the answers contained in the Christian revelation. Paul Tillich's method of correlation[2] is a case in point. He starts with questions which are implied in the human condition and attempts to correlate them with answers implied in the Christian message. The Bible for Tillich is an expression of the answers which revelation supplies to human questioning. Tillich in no sense identifies the Bible with revelation but finds in the Bible, and particularly in Jesus as the Christ, a picture of "new being" which is the ultimate answer to the haunting questions of human existence.

5. *The theologian should be aware of an assumed theological orientation.* This orientation will influence how the Bible is read and so will govern the frame of reference out of which to write theology. The traditional labels of liberal and conservative, though limited in value, do suggest attitudes and inclinations about the Bible and its function in the practice of theology. The liberal will be more inclined to exercise freedom in reference to traditional dogmas and creedal formulations and in the handling of the biblical text. The conservative will be more inclined to stress the inspiration and authority of the Bible and the value of classical statements of faith. Terms such as evangelical and ecumenical also have connotations which hint at the ways in which a particular theologian who claims such a label might use the Bible in the practice of theology. Clearly, the theologian's ecclesiastical tradition, be it Catholic, Protestant, or Orthodox, will also influence the way in which the Bible is used in that particular "brand" of theology.

Within each layer of tradition there are many smaller divisions; for example, in Protestantism there are a multitude of quite different heritages: Reformed, Lutheran, Episcopal, Free Church, etc. Often a theologian will have a particular doctrinal orientation and stress the centrality of one theme, which will hold a whole family of theological proposals together. Karl Barth's Christocentrism serves this function in the *Church Dogmatics* and determines how he uses the Bible. The controlling concept in process theology is an evolutionary view of the cosmos, coupled with the conviction that God is not only the supreme cause of all things but is also the supreme effect—God is affected by all that goes on in creation. This notion provides the eyes through which the process theologian peers at the Bible.

Circumstances of life and unique historical and cultural orientations will also shape the writing of theology. It is hard, for example, to ever write theology in quite the same way again standing on this side of the tragic events of World War II, the holocaust, and the beginning of the nuclear age.

6. *The theologian should be conscious of how the purpose of the work will influence the reading of the Bible.* Even as theological orientation affects the theologian's use of the Bible, so too does the specific purpose which the theologian has in mind. The purpose may

be catechetical and synoptic, aimed at assisting the believing community in understanding the essentials of Christian belief.[3] It may be polemical, arguing for the liberation of oppressed peoples.[4] It may be visionary, urging the church to play a more active role in the quest for peace and justice.[5] Or it may have a distinctly pastoral tone, providing guidance, comfort, and hope to the Christian community.[6]

Liberation theology, with emphasis on the need for the church's theology to better reflect the experience of oppressed peoples in third world countries, offers a good example of how theological purpose shapes the understanding of Scripture. Third world theologians, with the insight which comes from having experienced and observed oppression, are able to understand the Bible in certain ways which United States and European theologians cannot. The Exodus, the death and resurrection of Jesus Christ, and the kingdom of God are examples of biblical subjects understood in new ways as these theologians do the work of theology in reference to the theme of liberation.[7] The theologian may in fact find support for a wide variety of purposes and positions in Scripture. A text or passage is always understood in reference to a specific purpose, and thus care should be taken not only to draw out the full meaning in order to guide the church but also not to distort the primary meaning in order to support some personal point of view.

7. *The quality of a theological work depends upon the validity of the inferences that the theologian makes from the Bible*. Theology by its very nature is inferential. The theologian must bring order to an extensive amount of material from the Bible, and do so without forcing the material into artificial alignment. Sound theological conclusions grow out of biblical data, and any systematic arrangement of the material should be suggested by the material itself. The theologian must resist the temptation to draw too many deductions from any single text—to package the biblical data into neat and tidy categories which do not do justice to the complexity and quantity of the biblical data.

The history of the church is replete with examples of well-meaning people who have built entire theological systems around one or two texts. Certainly, one of the inherent dangers of the so-called charismatic movement is that too much emphasis is placed on speaking in tongues—so much so that this believing community gains its identity and character from this one phenomenon. The same can also be said for the Seventh Day Adventists who to too great an extent find their identity in reference to a day of worship.

8. *The quality of a theological work in some measure depends upon its open-endedness.* A good theological system is a growing one, one that is flexible and adjustable. As new data comes along, the theologian should allow his or her theological position to be altered and enriched by it. New perspectives on the biblical material emerge also, and the theological system should be flexible enough to be modified as it is informed by new points of view. Further, the church in each generation must deal with a new set of problems and concerns, and the theologian must be responsive to these concerns, providing theological guidance for the church as it endeavors to do God's will in reference to them. Theology is always an approximation. Further, it is also conditioned by time and therefore stands under the judgment of God. It is not God's Word but is judged by God's Word. As they become hardened into unchangeable orthodoxy, theological systems cease to be the servant of the church. To do theology boldly and with conviction is one thing. To do it defensively and inflexibly is another. The theology which is responsive to God's will and continues to grow as it is taught by Scripture serves the church best.

9. *Christian theology should be done in dialogue with the creeds and traditions of the church.* Creeds testify to the care and earnestness with which earlier Christians endeavored to state basic Christian truths derived from the Bible. The earliest creeds sprang out of the need to provide new converts from the Greek world sound instruction in the faith. Disputations and the permissive atmosphere of the hellenistic world made it necessary to provide a formulation of Christian faith which could be commonly affirmed. It is not surprising to find that the earliest creeds were baptismal creeds which were confessed by the catechumen when baptized.

In addition to baptismal creeds there were the conciliar creeds developed by various ecumenical bodies. The most famous of these is the Nicene Creed, or more correctly the Niceno-Constantinopolitan Creed, since it consisted of the original creed of the Council of

Nicaea (A.D. 325) and the continuing work done in refinement of it by the Council of Constantinople in 381. The church has not found it necessary to replace these creeds, but it has sought to reinterpret them by means of various new confessions which were conceived in response to the questions posed by new generations. A number of confessional statements, for instance, originated after the Reformation; new ones have continued to be produced by the church at regular intervals since.

The word *tradition* has a variety of meanings in the context of the church, but its primary meaning is the teaching and practice of the church distinct from the words of Scripture. Several early Christian theologians, including Irenaeus, Clement of Alexandria, Tertullian, and Origen, attempted to separate formally tradition from Scripture by "rules of faith." The Roman Catholic understanding of tradition since the Council of Trent (1545–63) has generally taken the line of claiming that unwritten traditions formed a second independent source of information and doctrine alongside Scripture. Not many Protestants would agree with this point of view, but all Christians should acknowledge that as a part of a living, historical, developing Christianity tradition is essential and deserves the attention of all who attempt to write theology. Certainly, it is through the eyes of one's tradition that Scripture is interpreted.

The theologian need not be bound by creedal statements and theological traditions, but to understand how the best minds have struggled with the important questions of faith can only enlighten and give invaluable perspective. No good theologian may dare ignore or disdain the theological formulations of the past. A host of able and sincere Christians have labored throughout the centuries over the implications of divine revelation. New creative approaches to theology can only be deepened and tempered by an awareness of the failures and successes of those who have gone before.

10. *Hermeneutics should be practiced in a way that correlates the text of Scripture with the current situation in order to provide guidance for the church*. This principle has been referred to several times already. It serves the vital functions of instructing the church on the meaning and significance of the Christian faith, assisting the church in a self-assessment of its fidelity to its God-given mission, and

pointing the church toward new areas of responsibility in thought and action. The maxim should not be understood so much as an attempt to limit the theologian's domain of investigation as a statement about the theologian's motivation and purpose.

These ten principles are not intended to be a comprehensive guide to or description of the work of theology. But they do represent some practical guidelines to aid the theologian in using the Bible to serve the community of faith.

In Worship

If in fact all good things come from God, then the Scriptures are surely one of the finest of God's gifts. They are given to the world as a source of history, wisdom, and aesthetic pleasure, as great literature to be studied, pondered, and enjoyed. But in a very special way they are given to the community of faith as a testimony to God's power and presence, and particularly to God's self-disclosure in Jesus Christ. They are not the sole possession of the theologian but serve the function in the life of the church of informing, nurturing, and guiding all people of God. They are a *means of grace,* i.e., a vehicle through which God's redeeming and sustaining love is made known and "brought home" to the people of God.

The author of the second letter to Timothy writes,

> But as for you, continue in what you have learned and have firmly believed, knowing from whom you learned it and how from childhood you have been acquainted with the sacred writings which are able to instruct you for salvation through faith in Jesus Christ. All scripture is inspired by God and profitable for teaching, for reproof, for correction, and for training in righteousness, that the man of God may be complete, equipped for every good work.
>
> (2 Tim. 3:14–17)

The writer no doubt has the Old Testament in mind as he thinks of Timothy, but his point is equally valid in reference to the New Testament. All of the Scriptures, Old Testament and New, are a gift of God to enable believers to grow in grace, to be people who are knowledgeable about their faith, righteous in their behavior, and spiritually attuned to God.

PREACHING

In every tradition of the church—and especially in the Reformed tradition—preaching has played a central role in the common life of the community of faith. It is one of the fundamental and distinctive marks of the church. Indeed, it would be hard to imagine the church without the presence of preaching.

In the New Testament the primary purpose of preaching was to tell the good news to people who had never heard it before (Acts 2:14–42). The word *preach* continues to carry this meaning, but it is now more commonly employed in connection with the preaching of sermons in churches. In the life of the church preaching serves the function of calling believers into an awareness of God's presence and truth. It is therefore an essential ingredient in the church's ministry to itself.

The foundation of preaching in the church is the Bible (Matt. 7:24). The preacher's responsibility is not to give personal views, hoping to convert the congregation to some particular version of current folk wisdom; it is rather proclaiming the word of God as contained in the Scriptures in a way that makes personal and significant its saving and liberating truth to those who hear, enabling them to apply the truth of God in their daily lives. It is not so much the preacher's learning, oratorical skill, or pleasing personality which makes the sermon effective (although these qualities are not unimportant); it is rather the Spirit of God using the words of the preacher to "make real" to the hearers the truth of the scriptural message.

The classical hermeneutical problem with preaching is determining how much of the Scriptures speak through the preacher and how much of the preacher speaks through the Scriptures. The preacher does have the difficult and complex hermeneutical responsibility of bringing the message of the Bible to bear upon the problems and conditions of the present age. It is not easy to "translate" the principles and insights of Scripture into idioms which are understandable and applicable in a world so different from the agrarian world of the Bible. To do so without distorting the intent of the text or using the sermon as a pretext to ride one's own hobbyhorse requires extraordinary care and discipline on the part of the preacher.[8]

It is possible to summarize the character of Christian preaching in the following three statements:

1. The primary *purpose* of preaching is to proclaim the word of God to all people whether they are believers or nonbelievers.
2. The basic *premise* of preaching is that it is based on the Bible, not the general reflections of the preacher about this and that, however profound they may be.
3. The chief *problem* in preaching is hermeneutical in nature, i.e., how to bring forward into the present the message of the Bible contained in the language and thought forms of the past in a way which makes it applicable to modern life and yet preserves its historical character and integrity.

One of the best ways to control the hermeneutical problem inherent in preaching is to be continually clear about the role of the preacher. When so many demands are made on the parish pastor, it is not uncommon for role confusion to set in. Insofar as the parish pastor is a preacher, though, there are a minimum of three primary roles to fulfill.[9] The first is that of *steward,* one who is the trustee and dispenser of another person's goods (1 Cor. 4:1). The preacher has the responsibility of "managing" the mysteries of God as they are contained in the Scriptures and "dispensing" them through the preaching of the Word. Implied in the concept of steward is fulfilling the responsibilities of caring for the goods which have been placed in trust. The preacher as steward of God must be faithful to the Scriptures and responsive to the sustenance of the household of faith.

The preacher is also a *herald* of a timeless message, not just one who manages it with care as does the steward (1 Cor. 1:21). The herald in ancient civilizations was one who was called upon to make public proclamations on behalf of authority. The proclamation was to be delivered exactly as it was received, without alteration or interpretation. In the New Testament the message which the preacher heralds is the *kerygma,* which has two essential components. It is first the proclamation of the mighty acts of God, and specifically the action of God in Jesus Christ. It is to proclaim that through his life, death, and resurrection Jesus has become Savior and Lord. It is also an appeal to the hearers to respond in faith and accept the message which is proclaimed. The preacher is true to his or her calling as the *kerygma* is faithfully heralded.

Still another word used in the New Testament to describe the preacher is *witness*—one who testifies in court to authenticate an act or event (Luke 24:44–48). If *steward* is a domestic metaphor and *herald* a political one, then *witness* is a legal metaphor.[10] The preacher as witness testifies on behalf of Jesus Christ in the courtroom of the world (Acts 20:24). Implied is the fact that the witness is obliged to be truthful in recounting the event being witnessed and to be persuasive in his or her character so that others believe the testimony.

Other metaphors could be used to describe the role of the preacher, but these three serve the purpose of capturing what it means for the preacher to be faithful to Scripture while at the same time proclaiming its message in an understandable fashion. The critical hermeneutical issue for the preacher, then, is how to preach in such a way that the past (the self-disclosure of God in Jesus Christ) is made relevant in the present, providing comfort and guidance for the people of God.

Each different type of sermon contains its own distinctive hermeneutical problems. While it would take us too far away from our purpose to examine all of these problems in detail, it is nevertheless important to make a brief reference to them. Traditionally, sermons have been classified by structure and purpose.[11] The structural classifications are generally three in number: subject sermons, textual sermons, and expository. Subject sermons are those in which the divisions of discourse are derived from the subject independent of the biblical passage. In the textual sermon the divisions are taken from the passage. The expository sermon is characterized by the preacher's exposition of the biblical passage, its material provided almost totally by the passage.

The recurrent problem in the subject sermon is that it becomes a vehicle for the preacher to advocate personal opinions and perspectives on a wide range of current issues. The text is merely a pretext for discussing whatever is on the preacher's mind, with little regard for the point of the biblical passage. The same risk exists in the textual sermon, although to a lesser extent since the divisions of the sermon are suggested by the biblical text. The danger inherent in the expository sermon is that the biblical passage is not made to speak to the problems which the community of faith is facing in the contemporary world. The dangers inherent in each type do not lessen their viability. All three have their place and can be helpful and effective in serving the needs of the community of faith. It rather serves to underline the necessity for the preacher to be careful to preserve the balance between being faithful to the message of the biblical passage while at the same time bringing the force of that message to bear upon the issues and problems of the modern world.

Sermons are classified not only by structure but by purpose also. In the New Testament the sermon was primarily *evangelistic,* with the aim of convincing the hearers to put their faith in the risen Christ. But as congregations sprang up the sermon also began to become *pastoral* in nature, attempting to provide a healing and comforting word to help struggling and confused Christians. The sermon may also be *didactic,* endeavoring to instruct believers on issues of doctrine and practice. Further, the early sermon was often *prophetic* in tone, calling the community of faith to its rightful mission in the world. Here again, regardless of purpose, the same hermeneutical principle holds, namely, that the preacher must maintain the tension between carefully handling the biblical text and yet allowing the biblical text to be heard in reference to the needs and concerns of the contemporary situation. This does not imply that the Bible is a resource book with ready-made answers which one can turn to for solutions to current problems. It is an ancient book, and no sleight of hand can change it into a guide for all of the problems and issues which face modern Christians. The point is rather that modern believers stand in continuity with the people of God in all ages, and the lessons and experiences of the past can feed and illuminate them as they attempt to live faithfully to God's will in the present world.[12]

LITURGY

The Bible not only functions as the foundation and source of preaching, it also acts as the center of worship for the entire Christian community. The liturgy of the worship service is full of biblical material, in prayers, readings, psalms, hymns, and sacraments. How this material functions in the church's worship also raises some interesting hermeneutical questions, chief of which is the way in which the biblical passages are understood by the worshiping community when they are used in the liturgy.

The danger here is that little or no helpful interpretation will be provided by the worship leader. When this happens, the meaning of the biblical passages employed in the liturgy often remains ambiguous, at best, for the congregation. As a general rule, the liturgical aspects of worship should be intimately connected with the sermon or homily, rather than the liturgy and the sermon forming two separate and quite unrelated parts of the service. There is little virtue in the mere repetition of a great deal of biblical material. It needs the thoughtful interpretation of the worship leader in a way which gives it meaning in the present day. This is not to imply that all the "mystery" of the liturgy should be removed by excessive explanation of the meaning of each passage or symbol. The power of the liturgy is preserved as it functions to enliven the imagination, and extensive explanation can serve to block creative imagining. The Bible is poetic and symbolic in nature and helps to supply the human spirit with the necessary images to sustain and deepen the faith experience. The appropriate balance is for the worship leader to provide the context for the biblical passages used in the liturgy so that the Bible is not misunderstood or heard to say what it really does not say.

In Teaching and Pastoral Care

It is not possible to establish an absolute distinction between teaching (*didache*) and preaching (*kerygma*), but it is occasionally helpful to differentiate between the two.[13] They certainly merge as the living Word is present in the words of teaching or as the sermon conveys information. In fact, the unity between them concerns the way the Word of God is heard through human words. Preaching, however, is prior to teaching in that it has the specific purpose of proclaiming the *kerygma*. The teaching ministry of the church grew up in response to the needs of those who were first converted by preaching, in order to instruct them in matters of faith and practice.[14]

The early church needed no special encouragement in the development of a teaching ministry. The example of Jesus as Rabboni (John 20:16) was before them, serving both as a paradigm and mandate. He was a teacher to his disciples and to nearly all of the people who had contact with him. He taught wherever he went: in the open air, the synagogues, in the temples. He gathered disciples to his side and privately taught them. As a recognized rabbi, he was often consulted on questions of ethics and belief. He used his actions as a basis for teaching also.

The Apostles, too, were teachers. Paul, who serves us as the best example, understood his mission in life to be an interpreter of the message of Christ to the Gentile world. In so doing he became the church's first and foremost theologian, teaching the story of the redeeming work of Jesus Christ to all who would listen.

The purposes of the teaching ministry of the church are obvious and may be summarized as follows:

1. *Understanding:* Some cognitive grasp of the essentials of Christian belief and practice is necessary for a full and vital faith experience. The more understanding, the more likely the believer will be to live as a responsible disciple of Christ.

2. *Discernment:* The early Christians were often called upon to live as a minority group in a culture which was hostile to their beliefs and values. It was necessary for them to be discerning about competing ideologies and value systems in order to hold on to their faith and preserve its integrity. The same is true today.

3. *Ministry:* In order for Christians to carry on the work of the church it is necessary to give special training for specific forms of ministry. Early in the life of the church, as a clergy class developed, theological education became an integral part of the church's mission. But equally important is the conviction that all Christians are called to ministry, and some form of education can only be helpful in the fulfillment of that ministry.

The use of the Bible in the educational ministry of the church carries with it all the risks of the undisciplined and uninformed use of the Bible in preaching. It can be made to say nearly anything which the teacher would like it to say and can even be a destructive force in the hands of a manipulative person. To insure the proper usage of the Bible in the teaching ministry of the church, it is as necessary as it was in the case of preaching and worship that the teacher preserve the delicate balance between being faithful to the intent of Scripture and allowing at the same time the Scripture to give perspective and guidance on current issues and problems.

Practices vary greatly in the use of the Bible in pastoral care. Different theological and ecclesiastical traditions suggest different approaches. No one pattern should necessarily be normative for all pastors. What is important is that the pastor develop a style that is comfortable and consistent, and that this style be sufficiently refined to insure that it is helpful and life-giving to parishioners.

There are a number of common objectives that all pastors share in the pastoral use of the Bible, regardless of the particular style of an individual pastor. In the church the Bible has extraordinary *symbolic* power, and the wise pastor can use this power for the well-being of the parishioners.[15] A mere reference to what the Bible says on a particular subject can be very influential in shaping the decisions of most people within the Christian community. Also, because of its symbolic strength the Bible can easily be misused by the pastor who may unknowingly attempt to control the behavior of one who is being counseled. An overdependence by pastors on the symbolic authority of the Bible, rather than a wise and sensitive exploration of its teaching, can be dangerous to the health of those who seek pastoral care. It is insight rather than legal mandate which produces positive change.

It follows that a second objective in the pastoral use of the Bible is to provide *guidance* to people who have serious questions about the course of their lives. Again, it should be stressed that the Bible is not a reference book supplying easy answers to all contemporary problems. But the Bible does contain wisdom and principles which can enlighten and inform modern Christians in their struggle to find answers to life's most puzzling questions. The pastor who has a thorough grasp of the Bible and who is able to draw parallels between biblical incidents and modern life is in a position to be of enormous help to those who come seeking guidance. The Bible does speak to questions of family life, divorce, sexual conduct, uses of money, and value formation, and the sensitive pastor, without forcing his or her views onto the parishioners, can point to these references as a source of guidance.

The Bible can also be used as a book of *comfort* to ease the distress and anxiety caused by life's small interruptions and large tragedies. Few if any of us escape pain in its many forms. Life's deadly enemies dog us, and it is easy to wilt under their pressure. Loneliness, depression, broken relationships, lost jobs, illness, financial insecurity, anxiety about the future, the death of loved ones, and a multitude of other experiences infest our lives with uncommon regularity. The Bible can be used by the thoughtful pastor to relieve pain and give new hope to those suffering from distress. By careful selection of appropriate passages and by a sensitive introduction of them into the counseling situation, the pastor makes the wisdom and insight of Scripture available as a healing balm. Of course the Bible can be misused by the pastor in the counseling situation. To suggest that it says or promises what it does not and to provide too much support, which enables the one counseled to avoid the responsibilities of mature adult life, are two damaging but not uncommon practices.

Above all, the pastor should not consciously distort the meaning of a biblical passage under the pressure of providing much-needed guidance and comfort. To be true to the biblical text while drawing out its healing insights for the parishioner is the key to the effective use of the Bible in pastoral care. But to promise more than can be delivered through a faulty interpretation of the Bible can only lead to ultimate disillusionment.

In Spiritual Formation and Ethical Decision Making

A widely accepted belief among Christians of all persuasions is that it is possible to hear God's word through the reading of Scripture. Individual Christians use the Bible in their personal lives to cultivate spiritual vitality and to gain direction for life's decisions. On the basis of this assumption, individual Christians have been encouraged to make it a daily practice to read the Bible. Many denominations provide daily readings for church members, and an endless number of devotional booklets containing Bible passages with some commentary, especially in certain seasons of the Christian year (such as Lent), are available to Christians.

There are at least three implications contained in the belief that God's word is heard in the reading of Scripture. The first is that it is possible to have *fellowship* with God through the Scriptures. It is possible to "make contact" with God, to communicate and develop a relationship with God by a regular exposure to the Bible. The relationship with God, in some ways analogous to a human relationship, needs the continual cultivation of exposure and communication. This notion which is at the heart of genuine piety is often expressed in terms of feeling close to God or sensing divine presence. It is closely linked to prayer; and often the Bible is used as a source for the utterance of a prayer. The many prayers contained in the Bible, including the Psalms, the Lord's Prayer, and the prayers recorded in the epistles of Paul, are an invaluable aid in the sustenance of a vital contact with God.

Secondly, the belief that God's word is heard in the reading of scripture implies that *insight* is gained which encourages growth toward maturity. To say it more "theologically," a regular exposure to the Bible enables Christians to move toward becoming all that God intends for them to be. God's word is heard by the individual Christian in terms of the specific needs and challenges of personal growth and development, in order that the person of God "may be complete, equipped for every good work" (2 Tim. 3:17).

Finally, the Christian who hears God's word through the Bible finds *direction* for the decisions of daily life. Life does present us with a multitude of options. We are bombarded with overchoice, and it is not easy to discover God's will as we run full speed through the maze of life. We know that the decisions we make have enormous ramifications for our future well-being, and for that of those for whom we care, and so seemingly sometimes out of desperation we seek to know God's will, believing that only in finding and doing it will we experience the best of life. The Christian turns to the Bible for guidance, not as an escape from the stress of decision making but out of a sincere desire to find universal principles which point toward God's will.

The primary risk for individual Christians as they use the Bible as a source of spiritual development is that they will not be able to distinguish between the voice of God and the many inner voices of psychic need. Some caution must be exercised in order to avoid slipping into an overly subjective interpretation of Scripture. It is true that the divine Word comes to us how and when God chooses, but it is hard to imagine God speaking a message through the words of Scripture that is unrelated to those words.

The Christian seeks God's will in the decisions of daily life and consults the Bible to find principles which are germane. Individual believers also look to the Scriptures for guidance for those decisions that have a specifically ethical character about them. The Scriptures are "profitable . . . for training in righteousness" (2 Tim. 3:16). All Christians are confronted daily with decisions that have ethical implications. The classic question of what I should do recurs with discomforting regularity. In what sense does the Bible offer help for those stressed by the need to make ethical decisions?

A part of the answer lies in the general principles that are articulated with clarity in the Bible. To love God and neighbor, to seek peace and justice, and to speak and live the truth are universal ethical norms which span the centuries; these values are not limited to a particular cultural framework. These universal norms, summarized in several places in the Bible (e.g., in the Ten Commandments or the Sermon on the Mount), provide helpful parameters for those eager to live in accord with God's will.

The Bible also contains a number of specific injunctions about human behavior. For example, the law portions of the Pentateuch and many sections of Paul's letters (e.g., 1 Thess. 5:14–22) contain "commands" which call upon believers to act in obedience to them. Some commands in Scripture are clearly contextual and have little bearing on modern life, but a great many touch sensitive areas of human behavior and issue a call for obedience to all Christians.

The complex hermeneutical issue in reference to both the general principles and the specific injunctions is how they "translate" into modern life. In what sense do contemporary Christians hear God's word in them? Each individual Christian must develop an answer to this question, and the answer will no doubt be influenced by the assumptions that are held in reference to the Bible and the particular circumstances of one's life. But even allowing for great individual differences the Christian should be open to having God's Word in these words of Scripture. To ponder them, debate them, and struggle with their relevance is certainly in order, but to ignore them or write them off as anachronistic is to run the risk of failing to hear God speak.

Hermeneutical Maxims for Using the Bible in Christian Nurture

The Bible is a primary resource in Christian ministry. It is used regularly and extensively by those engaged in assisting Christians to "grow in grace." Through the Bible God's Word is heard by individual believers and by the community of faith. It is God's Word which engenders new life and empowers Christians to be God's people in the world.

Because of the Bible's centrality and importance in Christian ministry, it is essential that the book is used by those engaged in Christian ministry in a way which maximizes the opportunity for its message to be heard. It is also important to note that in the area of Christian ministry there is the very real possibility of misuse of the Bible, in part because of the enormity and variety of demands placed upon those actively engaged in ministry. The following hermeneutical maxims should guide those who use the Bible in ministry.

1. The basic hermeneutical principles suggested in chapter five should be followed as a text or passage is interpreted for use in ministry. This practice insures that the primary and obvious meaning of the text will be understood by the parishioner or congregation. As the biblical author's intended meaning is grasped by believers, it becomes possible for them to begin to draw parallels to their own situation.

2. The minister has a special responsibility to draw out the particular meaning of a text or passage for the circumstances of an individual believer or congregation. This requires that the minister handle the text with extreme care, avoiding any distortion of its historical character yet finding an insight or principle which can be transferred into the contemporary situation. The foundational as-

sumption behind this practice is that the Scriptures testify to the way God has been at work with the faithful, and that God continues to work in and through believers in the present as in the past. There is continuity across the centuries in the way God relates to humankind.

3. Those who use the Bible as a resource in ministry have the obligation to be open and truthful about the history, structure, and content of the Bible. It is not necessary for every believer to be exposed to all of the complexities of biblical scholarship, but when questions do arise about the Bible the minister should give a straightforward answer. There is no reason to "protect" parishioners from the historical problems which arise in the study of the Bible. Indeed, the Bible becomes a much more understandable and helpful book as its history becomes more clearly understood. The same principle holds for the subject matter of the Bible. There is always the danger of oversimplification and other related forms of distortion. The Bible is a complex book dealing with the most fundamental questions of human life; thus it must be interpreted and communicated with the subtlety and sophistication commensurate to the complexity of its content.

4. A closely related axiom involves the humility about one's ability to supply *the* or even *a* definitive interpretation for every text or passage. To be self-aware about how much one's own preunderstanding imposes categories and shades of meaning on the text is truly the beginning of hermeneutical wisdom. It is false to assume that anyone can easily move back into another historical era and culture, penetrating the mind and consciousness of an ancient writer and discovering unequivocally what that author intended. Careful historical study is essential and greatly assists in the accurate interpretation of Scripture, but it is not possible for the interpreter to fully escape the controlling influence of preunderstanding. This "touch of humility" is important in ministry because it allows the minister to continually return to a text or passage and be taught by it. If one's pattern of understanding is not rigidly concretized, the text can break through and create new and deepened understanding. As this circular process goes on the minister is continually renewed and thereby enabled to become more effective in using the Bible in ministry. This posture of humility should in no way limit the minister in boldly proclaiming

the gospel. It rather insures that the minister's understanding of the gospel will be enriched as there is a return again and again to the Scriptures.

5. Still another hermeneutical axiom for the use of the Bible in ministry is that the Bible must maintain a "human face." The minister should communicate the message of the Bible in a way that expresses concern for the health and well-being of individuals and congregations. The Bible's overarching theme of God's redeeming love for humankind should be incarnate in the pastor's use of Scripture. There is really no place for haranguing moralism, inhibiting legalism, or guilt-producing manipulation. The Bible is not the pastor's tool to control the behavior of others but a resource to facilitate growth, health, and active discipleship.

6. Another axiom (or more accurately, reminder) is that it is the minister's responsibility to be faithful in the proclamation of the Bible's message and God's responsibility to allow the proclamation to bear fruit. It is the Holy Spirit who uses the minister's efforts to enable individual believers and the larger church to hear God's Word, sometimes in spite of the way the minister communicates the message of the Bible.

7. A final maxim for using the Bible in Christian nurture is that the way the Bible is heard by needy people depends in part upon the spiritual vitality of the one communicating its truth. To some extent the "medium is the message," and the one who ministers with Scripture must as far as possible embody its message.

SUGGESTED READING

Bennett, Robert A., and D. C. Edwards. *The Bible for Today's Church.* New York: Seabury, 1979.

Broadus, John A. *On the Preparation and Delivery of Sermons.* New York: Harper and Row, 1944.

Brown, Robert McAfee. *Reading the Bible Through Third World Eyes.* Philadelphia: Westminster, 1984.

Browning, Don S., ed. *Practical Theology: The Emerging Field in Theology, Church, and World.* San Francisco: Harper and Row, 1983.

———. *Religious Ethics and Pastoral Care.* Philadelphia: Fortress, 1983.

Capps, Donald. *Pastoral Care and Hermeneutics.* Philadelphia: Fortress, 1984.

Glen, J. Stanley. *The Recovery of the Teaching Ministry.* Philadelphia: Westminster, 1960.
Kelsey, David H. *The Uses of Scripture in Recent Theology.* Philadelphia: Fortress, 1975.
Nineham, Dennis. *The Use and Abuse of the Bible*. London: Unwin, 1976.
Oates, Wayne E. *The Bible in Pastoral Care*. Philadelphia: Westminster, 1953.
Oden, Thomas C. *Care of Souls in the Classic Tradition*. Philadelphia: Fortress, 1984.
Stott, John R. W. *The Preacher's Portrait*. Grand Rapids: Eerdmans, 1961.

III

Hermeneutics in the Life of the Church

Over the centuries, faithful believers have sought to understand the Bible and to make its saving message known. Others, motivated more by the need to understand, have probed the meaning of the Bible and attempted to explain its structure and content. Always there is a hermeneutical posture, a guiding principle or set of axioms, sometimes explicit though more often only implicit, governing this interpretive effort. There has been a remarkable variety of approaches and results, and the following section is an effort to present representative samples of these interpretative approaches to the Bible.

7

The Classical Approach: Origen and the Allegorical Method

Preliminary Considerations

Section I purposed to examine the fundamental issues that arise in any effort to interpret the Bible. One pivotal theme was the role of the interpreter's preunderstanding in the hermeneutical endeavor. Conclusions centered on the conviction that a respect for history and a posture of faith were essential prerequisites for an adequate interpretation of the Bible within the context of the church.

In Section II, attention turned to the practice of hermeneutics. There was first an examination of the role of assumption and methodology in the task of interpretation. The discussion then turned to the nature of the biblical literature and the ways in which this literature is used in "doing" theology and in practicing church ministry. Throughout the section emphasis on the controlling influence of the interpreter's preunderstanding and the need to preserve the two hermeneutical prerequisites of faith and history persistently remained in the foreground.

The purpose of Section III is to examine some of the hermeneutical approaches of representative interpreters of the Bible. These individuals have been selected as paradigmatic because they were instrumental in determining and articulating the dominant trends of a particular historical era. Each has also exercised a substantial influence on subsequent efforts to understand the Bible, and more broadly the Christian faith.

The interpretation of Scripture is the primary link between the ongoing faith of the church and the documents that give testimony and impetus to that faith. In every age the church has found it necessary to restate the limits of this essential bond, drawing out the implications of Scripture for the needs and concerns of its own particular time and place. This task is a function of interpretation, and the story of how it has been done is a complex and interesting one. It is beyond our scope to retell it in any detail here, but it has been recounted well enough elsewhere for any who are interested.[1] Our concern in the subsequent pages is rather to introduce the reader to carefully selected characters in this ongoing story. Before we meet the first one, though, it is important to remark again of the inevitability of preunderstanding's influence on any interpreter of the Bible from any age. To quote Karl Barth:

> No one is in a position, objectively and abstractly, merely to observe and present what is there. For how can he do so without at the same time reflecting upon and interpreting what is there? No one copies without making this transition. In affirming and representing what is written, and what is because of what is written, we accompany what is written, and what is because of what is written, with our own thinking.[2]

The concepts of faith and history will be used as a means of judging the adequacy of the hermeneutical positions to be discussed. Hans Küng writes:

> Christian faith can reveal new depths, perhaps the decisive depth, to the scholar. History entirely free of presuppositions is *a priori* impossible. But internal involvement promotes understanding. On the other hand a knowledge of history can reveal new prospects to the Christian believer, can give him insights and satisfaction, can inspire him in a variety of ways. Enlightenment—as history proves—can avert religious fanaticism and intolerance. Only faith and knowledge combined—a faith that knows and a knowledge that believes—are capable today of understanding the true Christ in his breadth and depth.[3]

The first biblical interpreter to be considered is the brilliant Alexandrian teacher of the third century, Origen, whose genius was devoted in great degree to the development of an adequate view of biblical hermeneutics for his time. There were many other interpreters and schools of interpretation preceding Origen,[4] but excluding Paul, he is in many ways the church's first great biblical scholar.

The Formation of Origen's Thought

Origen's thought was shaped during the first fifty years of the third century—an era in which potent fermentation of ideas and bitter rivalries between opposing ideologies were rule instead of exception. Assorted syncretistic religious cults which sprang up in Egypt, Babylon, Persia, Syria, and Asia Minor were blossoming forth throughout the Roman Empire. For the sophisticated, philosophy was readily available. The Stoics were active, as were Plutarch and his followers. Each group spread the influence and popularity of philosophical thought.

Of special significance were the various gnostic sects under the leadership of such people as Basilides and his son Isidorus, Valentinus, and his disciples Ptolemaeus and Heracleon. The gnostics dealt with religious subjects such as God and providence, human nature, the origin and destiny of the cosmos, Christology, and redemption. As certain gnostic sects seceded from the church their exegeses became more speculative, incorporating various expiatory rites, formulas for salvation, and asceticism from the syncretistic religions. The church too had its spokespersons who brimmed over with radical new ideas to be tried. Apologists such as Aristides, Justin, Tatian, and others arose to vigorously defend the faith. Intellectually, this era was far from dull, as these four streams of thought—syncretistic religion, philosophy, gnosticism, and Christianity—each vied to win the day for their cause.

The crucial problems which preoccupied this era were essentially religious ones. Yet the framework in which solutions were being sought was classical culture. The result was often a strange intermingling of new beliefs and religious mysticism with classical values and philosophical thought.[5] As we will observe, Origen's thought was no exception to this general pattern.

The city of Alexandria was in many ways the center of this ideological ferment. Nearly all of the main currents of thought met and mingled in this cosmopolitan and learned city, where schools, libraries, and museums were common features taken for granted by all citizens. There were numerous professorships of philosophy, rhetoric, and literature; the Ptolemies organized regular scientific expeditions; courses teaching mathematics, astronomy, and geography abounded. Toleration thrived also in such an intellectual atmosphere. Adherents of different cults and creeds lived side by side in mutual good will and inevitably absorbed bits of one another's point of view. As a consequence a mutual interdependence of Christian and pagan speculation was a most pronounced feature of the age. In this environment, Origen was able to gain an encyclopaedic knowledge, and he, like others of his time, assimilated more than one strand of thought into his philosophical and theological outlook.

Origen was born in or near Alexandria about A.D. 185.[7] His parents, if not Christian at the time of Origen's birth, were soon converted, and Origen grew up in a Christian family. His father, Leonides, was a man of means and culture and personally supervised Origen's early education which included nearly every facet of Greek learning as well as moral and spiritual subjects and the study of the Bible. Later Origen became a pupil of Clement at the Catechetical School of the Church of Alexandria.

When Origen was seventeen his father was arrested and ultimately martyred in the persecution of Severus (A.D. 202). Origen felt the impact of his father's death very keenly and wished to follow him in martyrdom.[8] Fortunately, he was prevented from doing so by his mother. One result of the persecution in which Origen's father was martyred was the flight of Clement from Alexandria and the consequent breakup of the Catechetical School. In a surprising move the bishop, Demetrius, put Origen, still a youth of eighteen, in charge. The decision proved a wise one, and Origen's course in life as the premier educator of his day was set. He soon attracted many students, not alone because of his teaching skills[9] but also because of the quality and character of his life.[10]

Origen's life as an educator may be conveniently divided into two parts. The first, 203–232, centered in Alexandria where he was an increasing success as a teacher and won pupils from varying persuasions and backgrounds. In the early years Origen himself taught the preparatory courses of dialectics, physics, mathematics, geometry, and astronomy, as well as the more advanced courses in Greek philosophy and speculative theology. Later the teaching of the preparatory courses became too heavy a burden, and he assigned them to his pupil Heracles. In addition to his teaching, Origen also found time to attend the lectures of Ammonius Saccas, the famous founder of Neoplatonism, and was influenced by his cosmology and psychology as well as his theological method.[11]

The second part of Origen's teaching career began in 232. After a controversy which resulted in his excommunication by the bishop of Alexandria, Origen was invited to found a new school of theology in Caesarea. This school which Origen presided over for twenty years was nearly as successful as the one in Alexandria. The courses of instruction were similar. After a brief philosophical orientation the students proceeded to study logic, natural science, geometry, and astronomy; for the more advanced, there were then courses in ethics and theology. At the outbreak of the Decian persecution (249–251) Origen was arrested and severely tortured. As a result of these tortures his health was broken, and he died in Tyre in A.D. 253.

Throughout his life, Origen was a disciplined scholar. In both the quality and quantity of his output he has had few peers in the history of the church. Many of his writings have been lost or destroyed due to later controversies that raged over his teaching, but more than enough have been preserved to appreciate the scope and depth of Origen's contribution. Martin Marty writes,

> Origen . . . inspires a gasp of awe for his breadth and depth of thought; he was a universal genius, a theological Leonardo da Vinci at home in philosophy, dogma, apology, polemics, exegesis. Though he was later repudiated by some in the East, he is the eastern church's greatest teacher and, more than others, formed the idea-patterns in which Christian creedalism grew.[12]

With Origen, the church's intellectual life came of age. Before turning to Origen's hermeneutical position, though, it is a good idea to examine the essential features of his preunderstanding, and particularly those aspects of his preunderstanding which play a prominent part in his interpretation of Scripture.

At the center of Origen's consciousness was his deeply rooted Christian faith. Thus his faith in the God of the biblical witness was comprehensive in his worldview. Yet the specific content of Origen's faith, like that of virtually every Christian in every age, was given by the environment of which he was a part. It is this specific content as it informs his interpretive method in its ideological, attitudinal, and methodological components which we will examine here.

The ideological element in Origen's preunderstanding of the Bible was supplied in part by the tradition of the church. Implicit for the person of faith in Origen's time was the acceptance of certain beliefs about the nature of the Bible—beliefs that Scripture is inspired, that it is a unity, that it was given for a definite purpose, and that it should be interpreted allegorically. As a loyal churchman, Origen assimilated these beliefs, which he understood to be handed down directly from the Apostles themselves,[13] as part of his hermeneutical system. Thus much of what Origen says about the Bible may be understood as an attempt to produce a more coherent and self-consistent version of the teaching put forward by Christian writers of an earlier generation.[14] Origen is particularly indebted to the Greek apologist Irenaeus, and to his catechetical teacher, Clement. From these two men Origen received most of his fundamental ideological assumptions about the Bible—assumptions that constitute the major influence on his interpretation of the Bible and function consistently and consciously throughout it. These Christian beliefs, though, are rather dependent upon a wider philosophical idiom, that of later Platonism, which is also an integral part of the ideological composition of Origen's preunderstanding.[15]

Origen had great respect for the principles of Greek thought as tools to be used for the explication of the Christian revelation, but he was not uncritical toward them, since he thought they failed to make knowledge of God available to ordinary people. Greek philosophical thought, he believed, was guilty of tolerating heathenism, had no power to convert souls, and had little meaning for any except the intellectually elite. The fundamental Christian problem from the Platonists' point of view is how the soul attains that certain level of knowledge which transforms it into the likeness of God. Origen accepts this Platonic emphasis but recasts its logic (which saw the soul's ultimate return to its divine source to depend upon its *own* discovery) by postulating that the soul's spiritual progress depends instead upon God's own self-revelation,[16] a revelation that is contained in Scripture. Yet the influence of the basic Platonic principles on Origen's position, used perhaps somewhat less consistently and consciously in his interpretative method than the assumptions he accepted from his ecclesiastical forebears, nevertheless should not be underestimated. In fact, no other Christian before him, not even Justin Martyr, had been so close to a philosophical school of thought as Origen was to the Platonists of Alexandria.

The attitudinal element of Origen's interpretation of Scripture is essentially what one would expect of a Christian theologian of his stature. As one who stands within faith, he is open and receptive to the Bible's message concerning God's self-disclosure in Christ. As a scholar, he is careful, thorough, and honestly critical of that which does not seem convincing. As a loyal churchman, he is respectful of the traditions of biblical interpretation which were commonly accepted by the church of his time.

Methodologically, Origen's preunderstanding as it relates to his interpretation of the Bible is provided by the tradition of biblical interpretation that preceded him.[17] In the earliest decades of the church the only written authority which could be called Scripture was the Old Testament. But the Christians had inherited from Judaism the concept that God's will is expressed in the written word, and soon documents describing the sayings and deeds of Jesus (the Gospels) began to carry the weight of authoritative Scripture. This inevitably raised the question of the relationship between the Old Testament and these new documents, and by the second century the church was full of a variety of ideas in regard to this relationship.

Barnabas believed that the Old Testament had meaning as it was understood in terms of the Gospels, and his exegetical method was characterized by typology designed to extrapolate from the Old Testament the essential truth of the gospel. For him, history had little meaning: God's covenant with the Christians had always been, and thus there could be no analysis of the relation between old and new covenants. Marcion took the extreme view, rejecting the Old Testament completely. His position was justifiable only from within his own distinctive theology, which posited the existence of two Gods—the just God of the Jews and the benevolent God of the New Testament (or parts of it) who is also the Father of Jesus Christ.

Arguing against Marcion was Justin Martyr, who held that all of God's witness can be included in the Christian faith and that the only real difference between God's revelation in the Old Testament, Greek philosophy, and Christ is degree. His exegesis of the Old Testament is at once christocentric and historical, allowing the historical reality of God's relationship to Israel yet insisting that this earlier covenant points toward its own supersession in Christ. Irenaeus defined even more precisely the relation of the Testaments and also against Marcion asserted that the same God is revealed in both the Old and New. The revelation of God in the law of the Old Testament was real and valid for its day, but now God is revealed in a new way—in Jesus Christ. Both Justin and Irenaeus were able to take biblical history seriously and set forth the permanent value of the Old Testament. Yet more definitive formulation was needed, and it was to be found in the allegorical tradition of Alexandria.

In biblical studies, the father of the allegorical approach was Philo, an Alexandrian Jew of the first century who desired to reconcile the Bible (the Septuagint version of the Old Testament) with Greek thought. Philo was convinced that the best way to accomplish this goal was to interpret the Bible allegorically. Allegory, sometimes called prolonged metaphor, is a rhetorical device that calls for a "higher" sense of interpretation than the literal. It differs from a metaphor in being a veiled presentation, a figurative story with a meaning implied but not expressly stated. Philo distinguished two classes of allegorization—the physical and the ethical. The former refers to God and the nature of the world, the latter to human duties. Behind the historical or literal sense of the Bible is a hidden meaning fitting into one of these two classifications. Every word and letter of Scripture has meaning. The gnostic sects which flourished in Alexandria also were great allegorizers, finding esoteric meanings behind the obvious sense of much of the biblical literature. Origen's teacher, Clement, was the first among the Christians to justify and explain the meaning of the allegorical approach. Believing that all Scripture speaks in the mysterious language of symbols, he was able to find biblical support for his already formulated thought. Yet his method was checked by his insistence that faith in Christ, his person and his work, was the key to understanding Scripture. The Logos which spoke in the Old Testament can be understood in light of the knowledge that Christ has given. The methodological assumptions of allegorical interpretation Origen takes over and advances in his own distinctive way.

Origen's Hermeneutical System

There are at least four fundamental presuppositions in Origen's hermeneutical system: (1) the Bible is inspired; (2) it is a unity; (3) it was given for a definite purpose; and (4) it is best interpreted allegorically.

First, loyal to the ecclesiastical tradition of which he was a part, Origen asserts that the Bible is the inspired Word of God and not merely a human composition. Though Origen has questions about the canonicity of certain New Testament books and attributes more value to some books (e.g., the Gospel of John) than to others, generally he extends the concept of inspiration to cover all biblical books and every word in each book so that error becomes inconceivable. He writes:

> We believe that there is no possible way . . . of bringing to man's knowledge the higher and diviner teaching about the Son of God, except by means of those Scriptures which were inspired by the Holy Spirit, namely, the Gospels, and the writings of the Apostles, to which we add, according to the declaration of Christ himself, the law and the prophets.[18]

He explains apparent inconsistencies by assuming that one of the two separate events is misrecorded or by resorting to the allegorical approach. In the case of solecism Origen distinguishes between the external word, about which even the biblical authors themselves were aware of their own potential for error, and its contents, which must be uniformly and absolutely without error. The medium of inspiration is the Holy Spirit, who communicates the revelatory message to the author and superintends the writing without nullifying the choice of words. The evidence for the inspiration of Scripture consists in its acceptance by so many and on its consequent power in their lives. Further evidence involves fulfilled prophecy, apostolic activities, which bear the authenticating stamp of God's presence, and the inner conviction of the reader exposed to the truth of Scripture.

A second presupposition in Origen's view of the Bible is unity. Against Marcion, the gnostics who depreciated the value of the Old Testament, and the Jews who argued that the Christians had no title to the Old Testament, Origen asserts along with Irenaeus that there is an innate harmony between both Testaments—a harmony of law, prophecy, gospel, and epistle. In the Old Testament the truth is hidden; in the New this truth comes to light. The Old Testament is illuminated by the New, just as the New only discloses its profundity through illumination by the Old. This bond between the two is determined and sustained through the allegorical approach.

Origen, then, accepting the basic assumptions of his theological forebears, understands the Bible as given and inspired by God and as a unified whole. From these two principles it follows for him that Scripture contains nothing unworthy of God; its whole message must therefore be accepted. This leads to a third presupposition in Origen's hermeneutic, namely, that the purpose of Scripture is the communication of divine truth. According to Origen the primary objective of God in giving humankind the Scriptures is positive and didactic, i.e., to transmit ineffable mysteries about human existence, God, the nature of the world, sin, and redemption. The Bible is essentially a mine of speculative truth rather than a record of God's redemptive activity in history. In a kind of refocusing of the Platonic ideal of the lover of wisdom, Origen believes that the soul makes progress through rational activity in attaining fellowship with God. The product of such study is theology, which is an interior grasp of the divine mysteries and communion with the divine presence of God.[19]

Obvious implications are that Scripture must be studied as well as read and that its meaning, though plain enough at one level, is in other respects obscure and hidden. Origen thus stresses the "mysteries" contained in each inspired book but not always made explicit. Therefore, it is necessary to compare different passages and to use techniques of logical analysis in order to draw out the hidden meanings of spiritual truths. If the interpreter fails to grasp the full import of a passage, he or she is in fact culpable. Origen explains, "If some time, as you read the Scripture, you stumble over a thought, good in reality yet a stone of stumbling and a rock of offence, lay the blame on yourself." He goes on, "There is not one jot or one tittle written in Scripture which, for those who know how to use the power of the Scriptures, does not effect its proper work."[20]

A secondary objective of God in giving us the Scriptures in their actual format is negative in nature. Scripture's sometime allegorical form serves to conceal higher truths under the guise of a narrative of palpable things or mundane human matters from those not fit to receive them. This form protects the mystery of the King from the mocking of the heathen. That which is sacred does not belong on the floor by the table for the dogs. Moreover, the literal sense of Scripture is sufficient for the salvation and edification of the multitudes, who would only be confused by the complexity of deeper mysteries. For them *pistis* is enough; *gnosis* is unnecessary. The highest truth of the inspired text is only to be appropriated by those who go beyond the letter of Scripture to its spirit—the symbolic meaning. Origen writes,

> [since] the Scriptures were composed through the Spirit of God . . . They have not only the meaning which is obvious, but also another which is hidden from the majority of readers. For the contents of Scripture are the outward forms of certain mysteries and the images of divine things.[21]

An acquisition of the deeper knowledge of Scripture goes beyond the salvation available to the multitude to a perfection available to only the few.[22]

Thus, according to Origen the Bible is meaningful in two ways: as plain sense and as a symbol of higher truths. In this way Origen's Platonism is extended to his conception of the character of the Scriptures themselves. The Bible has an inner meaning that is only partially revealed by its outward and literal sense. As Plato saw evidence for an intelligible order in the harmonious motions of the visible world which was its counterpart, so Origen sees in the explicit teaching of the Bible reflections of implicit higher truths.[23]

But even though Origen firmly believes in the inspiration and unity of Scripture and in the relevance of the whole message for the present, he is not blind to the difficulties inherent in such a view, especially those difficulties which the text itself supplies. Since by his definition there can be nothing in Scripture that is unworthy of God, Origen, the apologist, is forced to find a higher meaning for certain passages which appear to him to be unacceptable. He is aware, for example, of the anthropomorphic references to God and of the prophecy not yet fulfilled in his time. He finds much in both Testaments that is immoral and unbecoming, and he refers to certain Old Testament laws as worse than those of the heathen. Some commands, for example those enunciated by Christ in the Gospels, are impossible to obey.

There are accounts of events in Scripture which if taken literally are absurd, such as references to night and day before the sun was created or Jesus' seeing all of the kingdoms of earth from a high mountain. Even the Gospels contain passages that contradict one another.[24] Why then, if the Bible is the inspired Word of God, do these apparent discrepancies exist? They are put there, reasons Origen, to act as signposts to the fact that everything in the Bible has a spiritual meaning. They are providentially placed to warn us that we are not on the right track if we pursue the literal sense, and to remind us that we must leap over the literal to the spiritual if we would truly understand the Scriptures.[25]

This solution brings us to the most important presupposition of Origen's position—that the Bible should be interpreted allegorically. By this hermeneutical approach he is able to reconcile the inspiration and unity of Scripture, as well as its putative purpose, with all its textual discrepancies and embarrassing passages. Stated baldly, for Origen, the Bible says one thing and means another. Every injunction and every narrative are really mysteries shrouding a secret sense which alone is of real value. This does not mean that in Origen's view none of the Bible is history, that no laws are understood literally, or that no records of the life of Christ are to be taken as historical.[26] There are only a few passages that have no literal meaning at all. By this qualification Origen shows that he is aware of the worst danger of the allegorical method—that it is capable of dissolving redemptive history into timeless myth. He has before him the example of gnostic exegesis, presupposing a radical discontinuity between the plane of history and the divine realm in such a way that contact was not possible. Origen stops short of this position, complaining all the time of the "heretics" who go beyond Scripture.

Origen does believe that all Scripture has more than a literal meaning, though, encompassing in addition a moral and a spiritual meaning which can be discerned by the allegorical method.[27] Origen, unlike Clement, is not content to accept the allegorical approach merely because it is the traditional way of interpreting the Bible. With typical thoroughness he builds a rational argument for its use. He starts with the Platonic notion that earthly things in general and sacred history and law in particular are the shadows of things heavenly and invisible. If God made human beings in his own image, the deity may have made other earthly things after the image of heavenly things. Thus by means of the world seen the soul is led upwards to the unseen and eternal. Origen's principle assumes an analogy between the Platonic conception of the human being and Scripture. As people consist of body, soul, and spirit, so Scripture correspondingly has a literal (historical), moral, and spiritual meaning.[28]

Though he is not always clear on the difference between the moral and spiritual and often fuses them, in general Origen ascribes to the moral the passage's interior, individual, and practical meaning; to the spiritual, its collective, universal, and "mysterious" meaning. In the parable of the mustard seed, for example, there is the seed itself (literal), the faith of the individual believer which the seed denotes (moral), and the kingdom of God which the seed represents (spiritual). In this example, there is no literal meaning of the parable, which illustrates Origen's dictum that "all has a spiritual meaning but not all has a literal meaning."[29] Another example of Origen's exegesis aptly illustrating this method of interpretation is his handling of the Song of Songs. In its literal sense it is a love poem. However, according to Origen there are also deeper meanings. At the moral level, the "Canticles" can be read as the soul's desire to be joined in fellowship with the Word of God. At the spiritual level, the "Love Song" depicts the church's longing for union with Christ.[30]

Origen defends the allegorical approach against his critics in two ways: by argument and by appeal to authority. His argument begins with the premise that the Bible is inspired and intended to instruct each generation in timeless truths. Therefore, it cannot be what it appears to be, viz., ancient history, geography, and ceremonial legislation of and for a bygone age. It follows that the only interpretive method which gives all parts of the Bible a contemporary existential relevancy is allegory. Origen's appeal to authority is essentially an appeal to the example of Paul, in whose writing Origen finds instances of the allegorical approach. Origen refers specifically to Paul's use of the crossing of the Israelites through the Red Sea as an analogy of baptism; the Apostle also gives an allegorical twist to the story of Sarah and Hagar. From these instances, Origen draws the somewhat sweeping conclusion that a mystical meaning must have been intended throughout the whole of Scripture.

There are three additional matters which need further elucidation in an analysis of Origen's method of biblical interpretation. First, in order to guide the interpreter who employs the allegorical approach, Origen lists some objective rules. Not all the rules he frames are impressive to our modern ears, but the fact that he makes the attempt *is* significant. Those that are least impressive are his instructions concerning how to find clues to the hidden meaning of Scripture by studying the symbolism of numbers, Hebrew proper names of persons and places, and grammatical oddities in the text. More acceptable are his rules on how to avoid private, unrestricted fantasy in one's interpretation. One does so by: (1) taking Scripture not piecemeal, but as a whole; (2) interpreting the obscure passages on the basis of the plain, comparing text with text; (3) checking with teaching of other expositors; (4) insisting on a christocentric interpretation; and (5) hard work and prayer.[31] Secondly, Origen emphasizes that even the utilization of these rules does not insure a correct interpretation. The interpreter also needs the grace of God. Origen explains:

> There is the doctrine that the Scriptures were composed through the Spirit of God and that they have not only that meaning which is obvious, but also another which is hidden from the majority of readers. For the contents of Scripture are the outward forms of certain mysteries and the images of divine things. On this point the entire church is unanimous, that while the whole law is spiritual, the inspired meaning is not recognized by all, but only by those who are gifted with the grace of the Holy Spirit in the word of wisdom and knowledge.[32]

Thirdly, Origen distinguishes between different levels of inspiration in biblical literature. It is true that in most passages Origen presupposed the similarity and equal value of all parts of the Scriptures; in some instances, though, he divides Scripture into stages and grades of inspiration, depending on the worthiness of each author: Christ expresses the full revelation of the Logos; the Apostles, however, while inspired, do not possess the same degree of inspiration as Christ; Origen further differentiates among the Apostles and certain prophets, attributing various levels of inspiration to each.

An Evaluation

The influence of Origen on his own time and on subsequent generations was profound. Although his views on biblical interpretation were seldom accepted without controversy,[33] they were nevertheless accepted and were gradually absorbed into the mainstream of the church's thought.

There is little question that Origen's hermeneutical system did have a positive role to play in his own time. In the first place, his allegorical approach served the practical function of making ancient texts contemporary and relevant in the life of the church. This led no doubt to some errors in exegesis, but more importantly it gave the homiletician a tool that opened up biblical material which would otherwise have been closed. It freed the preacher from the confines of a rigid authoritarianism and allowed life-changing messages to be drawn from the pages of Scripture. Kept within reasonable bounds, this is the preacher's task in any age. This may in fact be the only justification for using the allegorical approach in biblical interpretation, although such levels of meaning apart from the historical may be possible if the historical sense is not ignored or distorted.[34] More importantly, though, Origen's hermeneutical system also served an apologetic function, that of elevating estimations of the Bible in an age when it was under brutal attack. By use of allegory he was able to uphold the rationality of the Bible and of its message against gnostic and pagan critics. Finally, it should not be forgotten that Origen was the father of grammatical as well as allegorical exegesis. Critics are fond of pointing to his fanciful allegory, but far less frequently give him credit for being the first great biblical scholar of the church.

A lack of appreciation for Origen's gifts of scholarship by such critics, though, does not make their criticism of his work any less cogent. To the modern historically and critically minded scholar, Origen's allegorical approach is inadequate. Comments like Harnack's reference to Origen's exegesis as "biblical alchemy" may be a little unfair, but it is nevertheless true that Origen's imagination did work overtime on etymological, cosmological, and arithmetic speculation of obscure passages.[35] The unbridled subjectivism to which the allegorical approach tends to lend itself allowed Origen to find whatever suited his purpose or need within the pages of Scripture. Even his own close adherence to the guiding rules which he suggests did not prevent Origen from forcing Scripture to yield up whatever supported his own point of view. There is little in his system to check the negative influence of preunderstanding, and there are few who would want to vindicate Origen's disregard to the biblical authors' obvious purpose in their writing. To squeeze a spiritual meaning out of every passage which the author did not intend and to find symbols where there are none is indefensible. Certainly no appeal to Paul's rare use of allegory can justify such activity.

To sum up, from a modern perspective Origen's allegorical interpretation of Scripture is basically a failure to be truly historical. This is the case in two vital ways: (1) under the influence of neoplatonism Origen did not see the Bible as a product of historical development but as an intellectual source book for speculative ideas. Even when he was critical of its contents, his use of allegory made it possible for him to evade the historical problem; (2) as a result, he did not fully grasp the historical nature of its message. He failed to see that the self-revelation of God has occurred in history rather than in the realm of rationally conceived timeless truths. Origen's allegorical method of biblical interpretation is inadequate, then, because he did not allow "history" to check, define, and give content to his faith.

SUGGESTED READING

Chadwick, Henry. *Early Christian Thought and the Classical Tradition*. Oxford: Oxford University, 1966.

Cochrane, Charles Norris. *Christianity and Classical Culture*. Oxford: Oxford University, 1940.

Danielson, Jean. *Origen*. New York: Sheed and Ward, 1955.

Grant, Robert M., with David Tracy. *A Short History on the Interpretation of the Bible*. Philadelphia: Fortress, 1984.
Milburn, R. L. P. *Early Christian Interpretations of History.* London: Adam and Charles Black, 1934.
Norris, Richard A. *God and World in Early Christian Theology.* New York: Seabury, 1965.
Origen. *On First Principles*. London: SPCK, 1936.
Patterson, L. G. *God and History in Early Christian Thought*. London: Adam and Charles Black, 1967.
Trigg, Joseph Wilson. *Origen: The Bible and Philosophy in the Third-century Church*. Atlanta: John Knox, 1983.

8

Modern Approaches: From Luther to Schleiermacher

Luther in Context

The method of allegorical interpretation, most clearly articulated in the church by Origen, continued to influence biblical exegesis until the close of the Middle Ages. Although this method had been challenged at one time or another it was not until the Reformation that a major shift in biblical hermeneutics took place. The chief figure in bringing about this change was Martin Luther. Indeed, no grouping of case studies in biblical interpretation would be complete without mentioning Luther.[1] His life and views not only illustrate and underline the central themes of this study, they also provide the framework out of which so many subsequent interpreters of the Bible work.

Before moving directly to Luther, though, it is necessary to cast a backward glance and pick up the main presuppositions that guided biblical interpretation between Origen and the Reformation.[2] This will enable us to appreciate the historical roots of Luther's thought and the significance of the change he brought about. It was not long after the allegorical approach of the Alexandrian school had been developed that it encountered opposition within the church. Jerome, who had at first been an advocate of this method, later rejected it and began increasingly to respect the literal meaning of Scripture, a shift of position influenced by his contact with Jewish teachers. In fact, wherever the influence of the synagogue was felt by the church, scriptural interpretation seemed to move in the direction of literalism.

Such was the case in Antioch, where the Jewish community had been prominent for centuries. Respecting the views of the Jewish leaders, the Christians at Antioch criticized Origen's allegorization and rejected his appeal to Paul's use of it in Galatians 4. The Antiochenes maintained that Paul believed in the reality of the events he described, whereas the Alexandrians were attempting to deprive biblical history of its reality. Theodore of Mopsuestia in his *Concerning Allegory and History Against Origen* argued that since in the allegorists' view there are no real events, Adam was not really disobedient. How then, he asks, did death enter the world, and what meaning does salvation have? For the school of Antioch, the historical reality of the biblical revelation was essential. Though they did not deny the possibility of a higher meaning than the literal, they insisted that such meaning must be based upon history. The Antiochene tradition, with its insistence on the historical nature of revelation, was further developed through the writing and preaching of Chrysostom and Jerome, and this tradition would become one extreme of the main forces in the church's understanding of the Bible, counterbalancing the allegorical tradition.

Another strand in biblical interpretation grew out of the uneasiness still felt by many Christian exegetes in their conflicts with Marcion and the gnostics. These minority groups and later ones which followed also made appeal to the authority of Scripture, and did so convincingly. Interpreters within the mainstream of the church's tradition often accused outsiders of distorting the obvious meaning of the text. But as allegorization came to be accepted by the orthodox theologians, this charge lost much of its force. Church officials soon began to sense the need for some external authority which would permanently fix the meaning of Scripture. They found this authority in the Catholic Church itself.

In the church, it was argued, Scripture had been preserved by those who stood in apostolic succession. Tertullian of Carthage early in the third century was one of the first to explicate this argument, piecing it together from the writing of Irenaeus. In *De Praescriptione,* written about A.D. 200, Tertullian makes his case from a legal point of view, asserting that the Scriptures are the property of the church. His argument runs as follows: (1) Jesus Christ came to preach the truth of revelation; (2) Christ entrusted this truth to the Apostles; (3) the Apostles transmitted it to the apostolic churches which they founded; (4) therefore, only those churches standing in the succession of the Apostles possess the teaching. This authoritative tradition was refined by Augustine in his *De doctrina christiana* written in A.D. 397. Augustine was no mere traditionalist; he insisted that a good exegete must be philologically trained, but he held that in difficult and troublesome passages the interpreter should be guided by the tradition of the church.

There is little that is novel in biblical interpretation of the Middle Ages. Essentially it is a period of transition, from the old patristic exegetical theology to the partial divorce between the Bible and theology found in the writing of Thomas Aquinas, a divorce that Luther did not accept. The materials of biblical study remained largely the same. There is a dependence upon a chain of interpretations pieced together from the commentaries of the fathers and a reliance on marginal or interlinear notes called a "gloss," which had been added to the text across the years of interpretation. The primary method of interpretation was the allegorical, with its postulate of a fourfold meaning to every text of scripture.[3]

Toward the end of the medieval period Aquinas reasserted the importance of the literal sense of Scripture. He did not reject Origen's contention that Scripture contains a deeper "spiritual meaning," but in agreement with the Antiochene exegetes he emphasized that such a meaning must be built upon the literal. He further contended that exegesis is an objective study, not one guided by some inner space. Here Aquinas interjects the modern note that reason is an autonomous agent and can make judgments on the meaning of Scripture. This note, present in the biblical humanists (e.g., Erasmus) and in later rationalists (e.g., Spinoza), is also rejected at least in part by Luther.

Where Luther, and in fact all reformers from John Wycliffe onward, did agree with Aquinas was on the necessity of some literal and grammatical interpretation of Scripture. However, here again there is a difference. The reformers insisted on the right of the text literally interpreted to stand alone. There are not several authorities in the church, but one which stands over against even the fathers if necessary, and over the councils of the church. The church is not arbiter of the meaning of Scripture, for Scripture—the Word of

God—is the judge of the church. But when the Bible was placed in a position of authority in opposition to the church, the crucial question for Luther and the other reformers was always interpretation. Luther's preunderstanding of the Bible was shaped by his life situation in a quite dramatic way. The general course of Luther's life is well known; it is not necessary to go into it in detail here.[4] Because certain events of his life had such an immediate influence on his understanding of the Bible, however, it might be helpful to remind ourselves of some of these events.

Luther was born in 1483 to a lower-middle class miner's family in Eisleben. His parents were able to provide him with a reasonably adequate elementary education. At fourteen, he was sent to school at Magdeburg and later to Eisenach. There was little in these early years, though, to suggest the tumultuous career that he was destined to have. In 1501, Luther enrolled in the University of Erfurt with the intention of pursuing a legal career—a course which his father had strongly encouraged. At Erfurt, Luther was exposed by the progressive faculty to the nominalist philosophy of the *via moderna,* which included a study of the teachings of John Duns Scotus, Ockham, and Biel.

This new school of Catholic theology laid increasing emphasis on God as personal will and on sin as the expression and result of the rebellious will of human beings. There was a definite break with the medieval notion that within the human soul is a fragment of the eternal Substance and that it is possible for one to bring this divine endowment into union, fusion, and openness with the eternal Godhead by means of a technique of *exercitia spiritualia*. To this new school of thought God was in no sense "Substance" but rather personal will. Between this holy will and the rebellious will of fallen and sinful people there does not and cannot exist a natural relationship or substantial kinship. From the human side there is an insuperable gulf which separates people from God. What is alone possible is a communion or fellowship between Person and person, the gracious initiative for this communion remaining ever with God, never with the individual person. The person's very response to this communion of faith is in fact in itself God's act and gift.[5] Luther's exposure to the teachings of the *via moderna* should not be underestimated as a factor in the formation of his preunderstanding.

Equally significant in this formation was the sudden change which took place in Luther's life on July 2, 1505, when the wind and the lightning of a thunderstorm aided him in facing an inner crisis which had been building up for a number of months. He knelt before a statue of St. Anne and promised to enter a monastery. In the face of his father's anger he entered a rather strict order of Augustinian Eremites at Erfurt.[6]

Luther found little comfort under the authority of the Roman system, however, and continued to be filled with fear and doubt. Continually haunted by the question of how to be righteous before a holy God, he threw himself into the discipline of the monastery. He writes:

> Being a monk, I wished to omit nothing of the prayers and often overtaxed myself with my courses and written work. I assembled my hours for an entire week and sometimes even two or three. Sometimes I would lock myself up for two or three entire days at a time, with neither food nor drink, until I had completed my breviary. My head became so heavy that I could not close my eyes for five nights. I was in agony and all confused.[7]

Luther was helped somewhat by an evangelical counselor, Vicar General Staupitz, who urged him to study the Bible and to teach at the new university at Wittenburg. After a brief stay at Wittenberg he returned to Erfurt and assumed the responsibility of lecturing on Peter Lombard's *Sentences*. Still without peace of mind, Luther made a pilgrimage to Rome in 1510—a trip that accomplished little except to instill a negative impression about the papacy in him. Returning to Germany Luther resumed his study and teaching. Between 1513 and 1517 he threw himself into the serious study of Scripture, doing expositions of the Psalms, Genesis, Galatians, and Romans. By the time he was working on his commentary on Galatians Luther was making use of many of the tools and methods of the biblical humanists, and particularly Erasmus' translation of the New Testament.[8]

In another dramatic crisis, the so-called "tower experience," a further important change took place in Luther's outlook. Believing that he had come face to face with God without being himself annihilated, he suddenly grasped the saving insight recorded by Paul in Romans 1:17 that "the righteous shall live by faith." Luther for the first time saw clearly that righteousness had to be a gift of God, not a demand of God in the law. For Luther this was good news, and ultimately his apprehension of this biblical theme proved to be the turning point in his life. He came to believe this message was the true treasure of the church, though presently obscured by the misunderstanding of grace. Grace was not infused into the soul as a supernatural quality, with an admixture of works and merits, but a divine miracle that made possible trust in and communion with God. Luther became convinced that such a message must be preached.

At first, Luther saw no need for repudiation of the past, but gradually the practices in the church forced him to ask why this truth he had discovered was not at the center of the church's message and ministry. Finally he was led to question the entire medieval ecclesiastical and sacramental system. In October of 1517 the issue came to a focus in Wittenberg over the matter of indulgences.

An indulgence was a remission granted by the church for the temporal punishment due to sins already forgiven. It was dependent on the merits of Jesus Christ and the saints and implied a "treasury of merits" which had already been piled up, of which the head of the church on earth was custodian and dispenser. In the late Middle Ages, this practice had become vulgarized and commercialized by professional pardon-peddlers. In Luther's time, Pope Julius II had established a jubilee indulgence to gain funds for St. Peter's in Rome. This offended German sensitivities; and the way the scheme was carried out violated the idea of free grace which Luther had discovered. A Dominican agent, Johannes Tetzel, was the huckster of indulgences in the Wittenberg area and provoked Luther's rage when he offered, upon payment for a certificate of indulgence, full remission of penalty in purgatory and a share in the merits of the saints without confession.

On October 31 Luther used the door of the castle church as a bulletin board on which to nail his ninety-five theses. His objective was not to pose questions regarding the validity of the pope, purgatory, or even the indulgences, but simply to call attention to corrupt practices. "Whoever speaks against the truth of apostolic indulgence, let him be accursed and damned" (Thesis 71). But unintentionally Luther had "introduced a world-historical revolution" because of the distinction that he made between the Catholic sacrament of penance and Christ's words on penitence.[9]

Rome at first acted with semidetachment. Leo X could not see that a theological dispute between monks could have much significance. But the matter soon took on larger proportions, and Luther became involved in a defense of his thesis in the Heidelberg Disputation. There he encountered Tetzel, and later, the papal emissary, Cajetan, at Augsburg. Finally he was labeled a heretic by John Eck, and the debate became more heated.

In 1519 in Leipzig Luther moved to the logical conclusions of his indulgence thesis—namely, that the sacramental system with its emphasis on works and merits was wrong; that the pope could err and in fact was the anti-Christ prefigured in certain New Testament writings; and that monasticism, mass, penance, and merits were not the way to a better life, but perversions of the free grace of God in Christ. Rome countered with a denunciation and called on God to rise up and purge his vineyard of this coarse, rude German boar. Sensing that a denunciation was not enough and that he had miscalculated Luther's power and popularity, the pope later issued the bull *Exsurge Domine* which Luther and his colleagues burned on December 10, 1520, along with a copy of the canon law.

Luther continued to publish his views in a series of tracts; soon he was called upon to defend them at the imperial Diet at Worms. On this occasion, he pushed aside his last opportunity to recant, justifying his stance by reference to his reliance on the apostolic witness and the voice of conscience. Upon leaving Worms he was taken into protective custody at the Wartburg castle and proceeded to consolidate his view of Scripture. The remaining years of Luther's life were filled with preaching, teaching, writing, and guiding the movement which he had begun. He died in 1546. This biographical sketch will be useful in piecing together some of the main features of Luther's preunderstanding which undergirded the specific presuppositions of his hermeneutical system.[10]

First note that Luther's encounter with Rome forced him to face the question of conflicting ideologies regarding authority. Step by step, each new circumstance demanded that he clarify his own position. Did final authority on religious questions reside in the ecclesiastical institution with its power to dispense grace? Or did it reside in the individual conscience which seeks to know God's will as it is expressed in Scripture? Ultimately Luther had no choice but to question the whole basis of the medieval Catholic system and frame a new theological structure based on biblical authority. This new structuring became for Luther the ideological foundation of his preunderstanding. It moved toward comprehensiveness in its scope, and it operated as a major influence on his interpretation. It functioned consistently, consciously, and rationally throughout.

Secondly, his own personal religious experiences, especially his internal sense of being accepted and forgiven by God in Christ and his exposure to the teachings of the *via moderna,* with its emphasis on God as personal will, helped to mold his convictions concerning the central message of the Bible. This message, he believed, revolved around the matter of God's grace and human faith over against law and works. By faith a person apprehends God's gracious activity in Christ and is freed from the agonizing strictures of the law. By this conviction Luther elevated faith to a central place in his preunderstanding. Faith became that attitude which enables its possessor to insightfully grasp the Word of God contained in Scripture. It is this attitude of faith in Luther which is readily apparent throughout his interpretation of Scripture.

Finally, due consideration should be given to the influence of Luther's education and study, both in kind and amount, in the formation of his view of the Bible as a historical document. His training in the *via moderna* at Erfurt, his reading of Augustine, his years of biblical study and exposition, and his study and acceptance of the critical and exegetical work of the biblical humanists all contributed to the formulation of the methodology with which he approached the Bible. Scripture could not be understood apart from a study of the grammar of the text. Thus an examination of the historical context in which it was written became the fundamental methodological assumption of Luther's approach to the Bible.

Luther's Approach to the Bible

What is the Bible to Luther's eyes? What kind of a book is it? What does Luther assume about the nature of the Bible as he approaches it? We will examine Luther's approach to Scripture from three perspectives: (1) the assumptions he makes regarding the nature of the Bible; (2) the presuppositions that guide his interpretation of the Bible; and (3) his insistence on the need for faith in interpreting the Bible.[11]

Fundamentally for Luther, the Bible is an *authoritative* book. Rome saw no need to make any choice between tradition and Scripture. In opposition, Luther, however, asserted the principle of *sola scriptura*. He stressed the contradictions between the purity of the witness of the Word of God in Scripture and the traditions of the church. According to Luther, ecclesiastical tradition had superseded Scripture, and the hierarchy of the church, as the conservers of apostolic tradition and dispensers of the sacraments, had arrogated divine powers to themselves. As Luther saw it the question turned on this issue of authority. In the heat of the debate with Rome, Luther proclaimed:

> Unless I am overcome with testimonies from Scripture or with evident reasons—for I believe neither the Pope nor the Councils, since they have often erred and contradicted one another—I am overcome by the Scripture texts which I have adduced, and my conscience is bound by God's Word. I cannot and will not recant anything; for to act contrary to one's conscience is neither safe nor sincere. God help me![12]

Luther conceived of the Bible as an *inspired* book, but one must be careful here since Luther's view of inspiration was not what his followers later developed into the doctrine of verbal inerrancy.[13] Luther never worshiped the Bible. He treated the text freely, arguing with Paul and John and questioning the canonicity of Hebrews, James, Jude, and Revelation. He doubted that Solomon was the author of Ecclesiastes or Proverbs and refers to Kings as "a hundred times better than the Chronicles."[14] Yet Luther could say with conviction: "We intend to glory in nothing but Holy Scripture, and we are certain that the Holy Spirit cannot oppose and contradict Himself."[15] Thus for Luther the Bible is not a stereotyped collection of supernatural syllables. It has not been dictated by the Holy Spirit; rather, the illumination of the Spirit produced in the minds of the biblical authors the knowledge of divine truth expressed in human form.

What gives the Bible its authoritative quality and authenticity is its message concerning Christ. The Bible for Luther is understood as a *christocentric* book. What is new about Luther's position in this matter is the way in which the content of the Bible (Christ) is linked with its authority and inspiration. In matters of faith and conduct, the Bible is the sole norm and guide. It possesses this authority because of its divine origin. Yet the authority of the Bible is not imposed externally or arbitrarily but personally as we encounter Jesus Christ in faith on its pages. Paul Lehmann remarks on this point:

> The content of the Bible and the authority of the Bible are so interrelated as to derive the authority of the Bible from its content and to confirm the content of the Bible by its authority. The content of the Bible is its message concerning Jesus Christ. Consequently, it has divine authority. But this authority is not imposed from without. It is the authority of the Spirit of God by whose activity the record both came into being and is freely accepted by all who read and heed what it says.[16]

Finally, we should note Luther's view of the Bible as an *understandable* book. In matters pertaining to law and gospel its message is plain. In Luther's argument with Erasmus over the question of free will, Erasmus remarked that much in Scripture is obscure. Luther replied in essence that the fault, if we do not understand Scripture, lies with the interpreter. By continuous and solid study of language and grammar we can overcome major difficulties; what obscurities may remain concern only subordinate matters.[17] For Luther, "the Holy Spirit is the plainest writer and speaker in heaven and on earth."[18]

The implications of Luther's insistence on the perspicuity of Scripture lead secondly to foundational presuppositions concerning Luther's interpretation of the Bible. In his early exposition of the Psalms (*Dictate super Psalterium* 1513–1515), Luther was still employing the allegorical approach of the fourfold sense of Scripture. Even in this, though, he adhered to the principle that nothing in Scripture is to be interpreted allegorically, tropologically, or anagogically which is not elsewhere expressly stated historically. In the *Seven Penitential Psalms* (1517), he forsook the fourfold sense completely;[19] and in his exposition on the Decalogue (1518), he began to mock scholastic interpreters who, according to Luther, treated scriptural interpretation as a game. Later he said: "The school divines, with their speculations in holy writ, deal in pure vanities, in mere imaginings derived from human reason."[20] By the time he wrote *Resolutions* in 1518, he was convinced that traditional exegesis was wrong. In fact, Luther believed it was not only wrong but evil, because it was being used to justify practices and beliefs that Luther felt to be unbiblical.[21] Allegory is rejected by Luther except in those few isolated cases where the biblical author gives a special reason for its use. By 1518 the reformer was convinced that "an interpreter must as much as possible avoid allegory, that he may not wander in idle dreams."[22]

In place of the allegorical method, Luther substituted the *sensus literalis, grammaticus,* or *historicus*. There is essentially one meaning for each passage of Scripture, and it is to be ascertained by contextual and grammatical study. "Each passage," he asserts, "has one clear, definite, and true sense of its own. All others are but doubtful and uncertain opinions."[23] It is the literal or obvious sense of Scripture which is the guide for faith and Christian theology. Natural speech is queen, and thus superior to all subtle or clever invention. Clearly, the way to understand the obvious intent of the language is by having a thorough knowledge of the biblical languages, making use of all the grammatical tools available, studying the times, circumstances, and conditions in which the author wrote and observing the context of each passage to be interpreted.

Luther was even willing to allow that whenever it could be shown that any of his own interpretations of passages were grammatically untenable he would not cling to them, however edifying. He refused to fall back on the evasion that he was offering a special spiritual sense which the words concealed in addition to the literal sense. In accord with this insistence on the historical interpretation of Scripture was his principle that Scripture is *sui ipsius interpres:* Scripture is its own best interpreter. "And, indeed, that is the right method.

Scripture should be placed alongside Scripture in a right and proper way."[24] The Bible is not so obscure that tradition is required to understand it. Rather, Scripture possesses *claritas,* i.e., it has its own illuminating power.[25]

The meaning of biblical terms is not determined on the basis of their usage by Aristotle, by the fathers, or in dictionary definition but on the basis of their usage in Scripture. The more obscure passages are made clear by the ones whose meaning is obvious. Says Luther: "It is indeed true that some passages of Scripture are dark; however, they contain nothing but precisely that which is found at other places in clear, open passages."[26] Although Luther often applied this principle as part of his general historical approach to the Bible—comparing passage with passage in order to understand the historical situation and the author's intent—it is also true that he often used the principle in a more theological way. Each passage should be interpreted in light of the whole, which meant for Luther, in light of his understanding of the central message of the Bible, justification by faith. At this point, Luther had moved beyond the historical to the experiential. The tools of scholarly labors were not enough.

This, then, leads us to the third matter in Luther's approach to biblical interpretation, namely, that the interpreter of Scripture must be a person of faith in order to understand its meaning. In Luther, there is not only the scholar's desire to interpret the text accurately and faithfully by means of the best tools of historical science, there is also the believer's desire to search the text for further illumination of his or her own decisive experience. Exegesis is never merely historical. It begins there, but proceeds in faith under guidance of the Spirit in order to discover the redemptive message of Christ.

Faith is a necessary preunderstanding for an adequate interpretation of Scripture. For Luther faith includes both understanding and experience. One must comprehend the message in its totality in order to understand its parts. "For although an understanding of the words is first in order, yet an understanding of the subject matter (*rerum*) is of great importance."[27] Such understanding is not a mere intellectual grasp, though, but an illuminating experience. The person who understands is the one who has encountered God in Christ and who is justified by God's grace. The exegete who has faith understands Scripture not by the autonomous use of reason but by the illumination of the Holy Spirit. Luther writes: "Scripture is the sort of book which calls not only for reading and preaching but also for the right Interpreter: the revelation of the Holy Spirit."[28] It is only the person to whom the Spirit of God has been given who will be able to understand Scripture as a whole or in its separate parts. Without the Spirit no one will perceive anything in Scripture rightly, not even when one has the most intimate acquaintance with its contents. But the one who has the Spirit of God—anyone, not just a priest—is able to grasp the essential message. Luther did not always find this doctrine of the right of private judgment an easy one to maintain. In the controversies that surrounded his life nearly all his opponents appealed to Scripture to support their case. But Luther rightly preferred this storm of debate to the stagnation of enforced conformity.

The person of faith directed by the Holy Spirit is guided by one final rule, namely, "to find Christ everywhere in Scripture." This christocentric emphasis is perhaps the central feature of Luther's hermeneutical position. It is the gospel message which has been grasped by faith that supplied the key to the meaning of Scripture. The historical interpretation of Scripture is not an end in itself but a means of understanding the Christ who is taught throughout all the books of the Bible. In the final analysis, Luther returns to the christocentric interpretation found in the New Testament—a principle which supplies Luther with a criterion for judging Scripture. By faith the exegete can determine which passages effectively "preach Christ" and which do not. He writes in his introduction to the epistle of James: "All the genuine sacred books agree in this, that all of them preach Christ and deal with Him. That is the true test by which to judge all books when we see whether they deal with Christ or not, since all the Scriptures show us Christ."[29]

Luther then identifies Scripture with the gospel of Jesus Christ, not with the explicit contents of a number of books. He insists on the primacy of those books that speak of Christ; for Christ, the very Word of God, is himself the content of the Word of God in the Bible. Such a view led him to a typological understanding of the Old Testament and allowed a form of allegorical interpretation to reenter exegesis. But he never allowed allegorical interpretation to establish proofs of the authority of the church; Christ remains above all merely human authority. Thus Luther understands the Bible as an authoritative, inspired, christocentric, and understandable book. It is to be interpreted literally and historically with the best philological tools available. But such study is not an end in itself. The one who would truly understand the Scriptures must be a person of faith in whom the Holy Spirit is working to reveal the message of Christ.

An Appraisal

There is much which is commendable in Luther's views on the interpretation of the Bible: indeed, far more than there is reason to mention for the purposes of this study. We will content ourselves with calling attention to the way in which his views relate to our theme of preunderstanding. Initially, it is important to notice that Luther recognizes the necessity of employing a historical methodology in the study and interpretation of Scripture. He sees clearly that without a historical check, interpreters can make the Bible say anything that suits their fancy. Only a literal and grammatical approach is able to uncover the Bible's true meaning and protect against the negative influence of preunderstanding. Luther is also aware that it is impossible for reason to offer a detached and objective analysis of the message of Scripture. It is only the person with the preunderstanding of faith who is able to discern the Bible's decisive and redemptive content—the Word of God. Thus for Luther it is possible to correctly interpret the Bible only when it is approached in faith by historical study.

As Luther worked out this hermeneutical theory in practice, though, for all his genius he revealed himself to be limited by his time and place in history. He was a child of his times in his uncritical acceptance of the historicity of the biblical narratives. The tools, methods, and presuppositions of scholarly study of the Bible that he employed, though advanced for his day, were nevertheless primitive by modern standards. He was also a child of his times in his use of the Bible in argument and controversy. Failing to appreciate fully both the historical origins of the Bible and its historical development of thought, he often resorted to the proof-text method in arguing his case. Further, Luther was a child of his times, though understandably so, in setting the Bible radically over and against the church. His principle of *sola scriptura* was perhaps a necessary corrective for his time, but one that now needs to be viewed in a different light, taking cognizance of the fact that the Bible is generally understood from within the tradition of the church.

There is one final reservation about Luther's view that needs to be mentioned here, one in which the necessary balance between faith and history appears to be overweighted by him in favor of faith—namely, his christological interpretation of the Bible, and particularly of the Old Testament. The objection here is not so much one of principle as it is of emphasis and application. It does not necessarily violate the integrity of a historical approach to maintain that Christ is prefigured in the Old Testament. But to find him everywhere is to contradict the literal-historical principle of interpretation and to fail to appreciate the historical context and message.

This objection, though, appears insignificant beside the abiding value of his views. His influence has been felt by nearly every interpreter of the Bible since his time. It is true that rationalists like Spinoza, standing outside of the church and in an altogether different tradition, came under the influence of Luther very little—if at all. But biblical interpreters within the church, even among Roman Catholic exegetes (though partly in reaction), and more particularly among Protestant exegetes, have not escaped the impact of Luther's approach to the Bible. Luther stands at the door which ushers in the modern understanding of the Bible.

SUGGESTED READING

Bainton, Roland. *Here I Stand*. Nashville: Abingdon, 1950.

Bornkamm, Heinrich. *Luther's World of Thought*. St. Louis: Concordia, 1958.

———. *Luther in Mid-Career*. trans. E. Theodore Bachmann. Philadelphia: Fortress, 1983.

Chadwick, Owen. *The Reformation*. London: Penguin, 1964.

Ebeling, Gerhard. *Luther: An Introduction to His Thought*. trans. R. A. Wilson. Philadelphia: Fortress, 1970.

Edwards, Mark, and George Tavard. *Luther: A Reformer for the Churches*. New York: Paulist, 1983.

Fife, Robert H. *The Revolt of Martin Luther.* New York: Columbia University, 1957.
Forell, George W. *Luther Legacy: An Introduction to Luther's Life and Thought for Today.* Minneapolis: Augsburg, 1983.
Friedenthal, Richard. *Luther: His Life and Times.* trans. John Nowell. New York: Harcourt Brace Jovanovich, 1967.
Haile, H. G. *Luther, An Experiment in Biography.* Garden City, NY: Doubleday, 1980.
Koenigsberger, H. G. *Luther: A Profile.* New York: Hill and Wang, 1973.
Luther, Martin. *Luther's Works.* ed. J. Pelikan and D. E. Poellot. St. Louis: Concordia, 1958.
Robbert, G. S. *Luther as Interpreter of Scripture.* St. Louis: Concordia, 1982.
Schwiebert, E. G. *Luther and His Times.* St. Louis: Concordia, 1950.
Todd, John. *Luther: A Life.* New York: Crossroads, 1982.

9

Contemporary Approaches: From Schleiermacher to Ricoeur

Luther's Legacy

We have seen that Origen raised some preliminary historical questions, but his hermeneutical system and that of the ancient church he influenced took primarily the form of allegorical exegesis. It was Martin Luther who opened the door to approaching the Bible from the perspective of historical criticism. Luther's single major contribution was the introduction of an elementary form of grammatical historical exegesis, although at times his historical approach was too christocentric. In the years following the Reformation, Protestant Orthodoxy slipped into the practice of harmonizing biblical passages with dogmatic formulations, undercutting any genuine historical concerns. The age of natural science and rationalism flirted with a genuine historical approach, especially in the case of Spinoza, but more generally searched the Bible for illustrations of universal laws of human behavior.

It was not until the nineteenth century that a historical approach to the Bible reached a mature independence from dogmatic concerns and metaphysical assumptions. Facts for their own sake became the concern of the historian. In fact, the best historians became the greatest masters of detail. In their endeavor to ascertain the facts, historians of the age worked out a new method of handling sources centered in philological criticism. Each source was divided into component parts by distinguishing its earlier and later elements, thus enabling the historian to discriminate between the more and less trustworthy portions. Even the more trustworthy portions were then analyzed in an attempt to show how the author's point of view influenced the statement of the facts, allowing the historian to rectify any distortions. Thus in most cases nineteenth-century historians spent more time collecting facts than framing laws, diligently seeking patterns of coherence and meaning from those facts. The ideal of the historian was thought to be the ascertaining of the facts in cool detachment in order to discover what those facts were without passing any kind of judgment on them. In reference to the Bible, historians developed handbooks of biblical interpretation which set forth the new method of emphasizing a purely historical understanding. They argued in fact that this critical historical method was the *only* legitimate kind of exegesis.

It was Schleiermacher particularly who objected that more was needed to understand the contents of the Bible than the methods of this scientific kind of exegesis. He believed that in order to understand the biblical texts fully the interpreter must join literary and historical analysis with intuition and imagination. The gap between author and interpreter cannot be spanned by objective analysis alone. The critical historical method must be supplemented, then, by an imaginative reconstruction of the selfhood of the speaker or writer. This imaginative reproduction of the creative act by which the work was first produced goes far beyond the principles of philological science; indeed, it infringes upon the realm of art.[1] Such a movement need not discount the importance of the grammatical and historical, for the interpreter must know everything possible about the language of the author and about the total historical complex in which the author lived. Only by a thorough study of the author as one who is conditioned both objectively and subjectively by the language and history can the process of empathic interpretation begin. The oft-quoted statement of Schleiermacher bears this out: the "task can also be expressed in this way: to understand the text just as well as and then better than the author himself understood it."[2] Once this goal is realized, the interpreter is then in a position to get on with the real work of interpretation—to "divine" the meaning of the text itself by identifying with the author in such a way as to grasp the author's individuality and purpose. This act of identification is possible because every person has a sensitivity for all others. As Schleiermacher puts it, it "appears to rest only on this fact, that each individual carries in himself a minimum of all others."[3] Thus for Schleiermacher the hermeneutical task begins with an initial study of the historical circumstances and linguistic symbols of the author, followed by an effort of psychological re-creation or "divination."

Schleiermacher's contribution has widened and deepened the scope of hermeneutics by making "understanding" its central core. Both his scientific philological work, which gave new light on the way human speech is used, and his emphasis on artistic penetration, which encouraged a sympathetic and intuitive reproduction of the author's individuality in the interpreter, have had a profound influence on even those who disagreed with him.

Certain potential dangers are inherent in any hermeneutical approach which gives primacy to subjective identification with the author, though this is not to say that such an effort is not necessary in interpretation. First, in such a psychological re-creation it is extremely difficult to take into account all the differences between the historical situations of the author and interpreter. Even by granting the common elements of experience between the two, it is still virtually impossible for total understanding to span the centuries of disparity which separate them. These common experiences shared by all human beings do not offset the divergent outlooks and temperaments of people of different historical eras. A second potential danger in a psychological hermeneutic is that it would seem inevitable that the interpreter, in spite of a thorough historical preparation which Schleiermacher emphasizes, might still unconsciously impose a personal point of view upon the interpretation. There would seem to be an inclination to read into the author's internal frame of reference one's own feelings and attitudes. This leads us to a third possible danger—the failure to freely acknowledge that the author is not trying to describe and discuss his or her soul or inner life but a real subject, a subject that in fact easily gets lost with the emphasis upon subjective identification with the author. The implications of this for biblical hermeneutics become serious when God as subject is ignored or denied because of an overemphasis on discerning the faith or attitude of the author.

It is obvious that the role of preunderstanding in Schleiermacher's hermeneutical system is an important one. His own personal background and cultural and historical surroundings had their influence on the formation of the preunderstanding out of which he approached the Christian faith.[4] His early experiences with the Moravians, a group which stressed personal piety, and his later social contacts in Berlin and Halle with their emphasis on earnest and frank conversation embued him with a sensitivity to the subtle innuendo of nuances and tones in the speech and gestures of others. Also, living in the age of Romanticism he was made particularly conscious of the meaning and importance of personal experience and creative imagination as well as rigor in scholarly work. But what is even more important for our purpose is to see the place he gives to artistic sensitivity and proper attitude as a necessary "preunderstanding" for interpretation. The interpreter must have a sympathetic affinity to do justice to any given text.

A similar place is given to the role of preunderstanding in the hermeneutical theory of Wilhelm Dilthey. He too stressed the need to go beyond traditional hermeneutics by giving a greater role to understanding, understanding realized through an appropriate frame of reference with which to approach the text. For Dilthey, as for Schleiermacher, the interpreter must experience, or rather re-experience, the original creative moment of the author in order to do justice to the text. True understanding only comes about when the interpreter, after a thorough study of the grammatical, linguistic, and historical background, projects into the life of the author by means of an imaginative act and recreates the author's own life situation.[5]

> Understanding is a rediscovery of the I in the Thou; mind rediscovers itself on higher and higher levels of systematic connection; this identity of mind in the I, in the Thou, in every subject within a community, in every system of culture, and finally in the totality of mind and of the world history, makes possible the joint result of various operations performed in the human studies.[6]

Such understanding in the interpretive process defies exact scientific explication and can only be learned from interpreters of genius.

Although both Schleiermacher and Dilthey stress the need for creative empathy on the part of the interpreter, it was Dilthey who saw more clearly that historical events in the past must be read as expressions of historical life. The historian, according to Dilthey, is able to interpret the past because all historical events are effects of the human spirit, in whose structures and capacities all humanity including the historian also participates.[7] Dilthey, though, did not altogether escape the potential limitations of the psychological method either. Reducing the understanding of a historical document to the possibilities of common experiences between author and interpreter does not allow for adequate interpretation of the new and uncommon. These events are in danger of being ruled out by the limitations of the hermeneutical method. When it comes to biblical interpretation, all that can be heard is what common human experience allows. This would exclude the possibility of a unique revelatory act of God in history, an event that by definition cannot be handled in a psychologically determined hermeneutic.

The concept of preunderstanding also plays a significant role in the philosophy of Martin Heidegger.[8] Hermeneutics is first mentioned by Heidegger in *Being and Time*, where the phenomenology of *Dasein* (human existence) is called a "hermeneutic." As his theme develops, Heidegger uses two words which mean interpretation: (1) *Auslegung*, which is an informal kind of interpretation that accompanies every act of understanding; it is the frame of reference (*Vorstruktur*) which we bring to any situation and which makes possible understanding; and (2) *Interpretation*, which describes the more specific and explicit interpretation of a text. In *Interpretation* there will also be some preunderstanding that is brought to the task of what Heidegger calls the hermeneutical situation.[9]

Heidegger's hermeneutical position may be summarized in three phases which constitute a unity.[10] In phase one, the text is to be interpreted in terms of human self-understanding. Here preunderstanding is given a relatively important place. Phase two represents a shift away from preunderstanding to an attitude which receives the text itself as it confronts the interpreter. Here the interpreter has a more passive role. As Heidegger says: "Hence in interpreting [the poem under consideration], we must avoid not only inappropriate ideas of man but all ideas of man whatsoever. We must attempt to hear only what is said."[11] In phase three, Heidegger sees the poet as having a kind of direct rapport with the theme, and the language of the poem is viewed as the language of Being. The interpreter "listens" to the language of the poem as an actualized self-expression of Being.[12] Macquarrie summarizes Heidegger's hermeneutic by saying, "Language has to be understood as both an existential and an ontological phenomenon; interpretation demands both questioning and listening, a sense of direction and a willingness to be directed."[13] What is important to note about Heidegger's view of hermeneutics, as was the case with Schleiermacher and Dilthey, is the emphasis on an appropriate preunderstanding in order to hear what is being said, whether the message is existential or ontological, and whether we question the text or merely listen to it.

The interpreter who was and perhaps still is the central figure in any discussion of modern biblical hermeneutics is Rudolf Bultmann. Bultmann's hermeneutic has its foundation in Heidegger's phase one—viz., that the text is to be interpreted in terms of our self-understanding. The movement of Bultmann's method of interpretation, though, is away from language (of which mythological language serves as a model) back to an understanding which is prior to, and more authentic than, language.[14] The way to grasp the real meaning of historical phenomena is by analyzing human existence via Heidegger's philosophical categories. Bultmann's concern is to discover the condition under which any historical understanding is possible. For given the need of the interpreter to recapture the author's experience of Being and the gap of the ages, the question of whether *any* such understanding is possible becomes legitimate. This understanding, he believes, is available through the interpreter's relationship in life to the subject which is expressed in the text. As with Schleiermacher and Dilthey, Bultmann sees the need for a certain common element between the author and the interpreter—a common interest in a common subject. This interest may take on a different form in the author and interpreter, yet without a living relation to the message of the text the interpreter will never be able to comprehend it.[15] Bultmann writes, "The presupposition for comprehension is the connection of text and interpreter, which is founded on the life relationship of the interpreter to the subject, which is passed on by the text."[16] This relationship to the text, which Bultmann describes as preunderstanding, shapes the question which is put to the text and to which the text will respond. The preunderstanding which makes possible this understanding encounter with history may or may not be explicit in one's own experience of the subject of the text. The task of the interpreter of biblical writings is the same as it is for all other kinds of literature. The interpreter brings to the biblical text a preunderstanding and an openness to the meaning of human existence and proceeds to interpret the original mythological statements of Scripture in terms of the understanding of human existence before God which they adequately express. It is a question of how human existence is understood in the Bible. As Bultmann expresses it: "If the object of interpretation is designated as the inquiry about God and the manifestations of God, this means, in fact, that it is the inquiry into the reality of human existence."[17]

If preunderstanding plays such a central role in interpretation, how, then, is objectivity possible? Bultmann argues that it is because historical inquiry is different from scientific inquiry. The interpreter should not and cannot be detached, "For facts of the past only become historical phenomena when they become significant for a subject which itself stands in history and is involved in it."[18] Every formulation has the potential of leading to an unambiguous, objective understanding whenever the interpretation is systematically carried out. For Bultmann, to "demand that the interpreter must silence his subjectivity and extinguish his individuality, in order to attain to an objective knowledge is, therefore the most absurd one that can be imagined."[19]

The question which immediately arises, though, is whether Bultmann's concept of existential self-understanding is too limiting as a hermeneutical principle. One may grant that it forms an integral part of any adequate interpretive method, but when it is used exclusively as the only norm of interpretation does it not in fact censure the text? Does his commitment to the hermeneutical principle that the life of the interpreter is the condition for understanding prevent him from making use of statements about God, the world, Christ, and human nature as they are contained in the objectified language of the New Testament?[20] Is this not a violation of the spirit of biblical texts? Also, one wonders if his assertion that the Bible should be interpreted by the same method as other literature does not contain ambiguity.

Bultmann does accept that the Word of God is heard in Scripture; and in fact, as Gadamer points out, Bultmann does operate with a preunderstanding full of theological assumptions.[21] Perhaps the theologians should admit the possibility of a sacred and profane hermeneutic and acknowledge that in biblical interpretation a preunderstanding is employed which is conditioned by experiences and interests which are less than universal—viz., the personal insight of *faith*. Perhaps the category of human existence as the only appropriate preunderstanding in biblical interpretation is too narrow. And perhaps room should be made for faith as given in the community of believers which understands the Bible as primarily the testimony of God's redemptive acts in history and only secondarily, though necessarily also, as an explication of human existence.

Hermeneutics Since Bultmann

Bultmann's work in hermeneutics has been continued with varying emphases by a number of theologians. The so-called "new hermeneutic," for instance, whose central expositors are Ebeling and Fuchs, defines hermeneutics as the theory of understanding how the Word of God once proclaimed in text moves on into fresh proclamation, i.e., into a situation in which the proclamation can produce faith anew. The accent falls upon the reality that is communicated through existentially understanding the Word of God, removing obstacles to faith and engendering faith, as in the biblical text.[22] It is the oral character of this renewed Word which is decisive in producing faith or authentic existence. Hence the new hermeneutic is really a theory about words and what happens as an event through words.

For Ebeling, hermeneutics is the understanding of the Word of God becoming event again and again within the sphere of human language. He says: "Whatever precise theological definition may be given to the *concept of the Word of God,* at all events, it points us to something that happens, *viz.*, to the movement which leads from the text of holy scripture to the sermon.[23] . . . Whatever the precise definition may be given to '*hermeneutics*' . . . it has to do with the word-event."[24] Whereas Bultmann wants to probe beneath the language of the Bible to the understanding of human existence which it enshrines, Ebeling sees the language itself as the voice of being. *"The primary phenomenon in the realm of understanding,"* he maintains, *"is not understanding* OF *language, but understanding* THROUGH *language."*[25]

Fuchs also is concerned with language. He describes a human being as a linguistic creature who answers the call of being. This call is heard by human beings by means of history; for history is basically the history of language for Fuchs, of being coming to expression through language. The Word of God is the coming of authentic language, the language of love in Jesus. Jesus himself is a major "language event," and he teaches us the language of faith and encourages us to try it out in order to become closer with God.[26] Hence for Fuchs the historical Jesus gains renewed significance.

In both Fuchs and Ebeling, there is an attempt to find an authentic language through which the Word of God can express itself as event, producing faith and avoiding counterfeit language which objectifies human beings and thus becomes an obstacle to faith. In this "new hermeneutic," language becomes the key to understanding biblical text, rather than the interpreter's relationship to the subject of the text as was the case for Bultmann. But *should* language be singled out as the only legitimate medium of the biblical revelation? What, for example, happens to history as a means of God's self-disclosure? Once again, it would appear that the content of the *kerygma* as an object of faith has been obscured. There is little recognition that the crucifixion and resurrection are historical events themselves creative of language, not merely "language events." Language as the only hermeneutical guide fails to do full justice to history. Neither will it do more than a small part of the primary hermeneutical task of spanning the years which lie between the redemptive events and contemporary life, for these events come to us in many nonverbal ways, for example, through the sacraments.

In a slightly different formulation, Henrich Ott attempts to find a mediating position among Barth, Heidegger, and Bultmann. As student of and successor to Karl Barth, he inherited an emphasis on the Word of God which is clarified in dogmatics for the task of preaching. But the problem for Ott is how the Word of God is able to be understood in its proclamation. To this end he proposes that theology must turn more toward the human realm, to the human situation. From Heidegger and Bultmann Ott finds direction for this maneuver. From Heidegger he appropriates an ontology of human existence and language; from Bultmann he receives an impetus to shape his hermeneutic toward persons to whom the Word of God must be existentially meaningful. Ott works out the implications of these principles in his book *Theology and Preaching,*[27] where he struggles with the problem of how dogmatics is able to facilitate the movement from the Bible to preaching. He is concerned to show how genuine preaching is possible today—meaning by genuine preaching the proclamation which enables the biblical message to be understood in terms of human existence.

He employs the figure of the "hermeneutical arch" to describe the totality of this process of understanding.[28] The arch stretches between the biblical text and the sermon. Dogmatics to clarify the subject matter of the text stands between exegesis and homiletics. Philosophy assists it in shedding light on the concrete existence of human beings today. Thus preaching, built on the foundation of theology and ontology, is able to answer the real existential concern of modern people. At this point, Ott would appear to break from Barth and move closer to Bultmann's existential hermeneutic. Yet he acknowledges the danger of allowing a philosophical point of view to determine the scope and content of the dogmatic formulation of the gospel.

Wolfhart Pannenberg shifts to a new focus, attempting to find a solution to the hermeneutical questions in terms of world history. He defines the hermeneutic problem in terms of how a given content can be repeated in a completely changed situation. As he puts it: "How can the distance between the past of the texts and the present of the interpreter be bridged?"[29] The modern historical method of exegesis requires us to interpret Scripture in light of its original intention, and we are gradually becoming more conscious of the distance that separates us from the text. The solution, he argues, lies in the concept of merging horizons, a notion developed by Gadamer.[30]

This concept involves enlarging the intellectual horizon of understanding of the interpreter to also include the horizon of understanding of the text. This gap between our horizon and that of the text must be spanned without either being effaced. Whereas Liberalism tended to swallow the past in the present, Orthodoxy is inclined to ignore the present by emphasizing the past. A concept is needed that will give an overarching perspective. Pannenberg does not think that Bultmann's demythologizing and Bonhoeffer's nonreligious interpretation are adequate. In both, theology loses its object and ceases to be theology. Only *Universalgeschichte* serves as an adequate perspective.[31] As Pannenberg says:

> Thus the present situation may be related to that of early Christianity in terms of that horizon which alone connects both without blurring their differences, namely, the horizon of the *historical process*. The hermeneutical difference between the traditional texts and our present time would be at once respected and superseded in a concept of the *history* connecting both, if this history can again be regarded as the work of the biblical God.[32]

The key is in the last phrase, which describes history as God's unfolding plan for the world. One must speak of God in relation to reality as a whole, not limit God's domain. The biblical God is one true God who must be seen in relation to universal history as the ultimate horizon of reality. Universal history can bridge the distance between the time of Jesus and the twentieth century and make a solution to the hermeneutical problem possible.[33]

Jürgen Moltmann endeavors to find an answer to the hermeneutical question in the idea of Christian hope.[34] Grounding his view of hope in the resurrection, Moltmann develops what he calls a political hermeneutic.[35] What unites the gospel of the cosmological metaphysics of another era with the gospel of the modern world? It is human suffering—the chaos and absurdity of history and the threat of human transiency. The gospel, clothed in the myth and language of another culture, leaps forward into our time with a message of hope, hope that these conditions of human suffering can be changed. Through the proclamation of the resurrection of the crucified one new life is created. The gospel attains its contemporary as well as its revolutionary meaning. Moltmann writes, "The political configuration of the church and the ethical form of the Christian life are the proper subject matter of Christian hermeneutical considerations."[36]

Liberation theology also keeps the focus of the hermeneutical discussion on the church's contemporary witness. A "pure theology," deducible from a set of *a priori* principles—i.e., a self-contained academic hermeneutical procedure which leads to an intellectual conversation about the application of Christian faith to modern problems—is an inadequate starting point. The issue rather is *praxis,* the fusion of accumulated wisdom of Christian reflection with a program designed to change an unjust society into a just one.[37]

There is a fear, justified I think, on the part of liberation theologians that traditional American and European theology contains ideological elements which sustain bourgeois society, the class structure, and the misery of the proletariat. To discover this hidden theoretical resistance to revolution as an end to oppression is part of the motivating force behind liberation theology. A new ideological system, Marxism, is substituted, a system which is purported to uncover the vested interests of the present power structure of traditional theology. Thus, this new ideology becomes the hermeneutical starting point; the difference, though, is that this starting point is likewise the starting point of a revolutionary plan of action. *Praxis* retains its absolute priority.[38]

Process theology is another variation on the hermeneutical agenda, again highly dependent upon an ideology. Leaning heavily upon the metaphysical philosophy of Alfred North Whitehead, process theologians view reality as both temporal and creative and therefore stress "becoming," as opposed to Heidegger's emphasis on "being." The story of the influence of Whitehead's philosophy on British and American theology is long and complex and goes far beyond our purposes here. Suffice it to say that several important theologians[39] have attempted to appropriate Whitehead's vision of reality for application to cultural and theological problems and the development of theological systems. What is important to note for our discussion is the use of a self-consciously chosen ideology as a preunderstanding in the interpretation of Christian faith. Thus, Whitehead's particular metaphysical position becomes the controlling hermeneutic for process theologians.[40]

Another group of theologians, not of any one school or tradition, have attempted to interpret the Christian faith in independent though surprisingly similar ways which can be understood and affirmed by people immersed in modern culture. Their works are apologies for faith, and bear a hermeneutical resemblance to Schleiermacher's *On Religion: Addresses in Response to its Cultured Critics* and Paul Tillich's *Systematic Theology* with its "correlation" hermeneutic. Hans Küng's *On Being a Christian,*[41] widely read and discussed, is representative. Drawing upon current social and political themes, on trends in western culture, and on what he calls the "humanization of man," Küng endeavors to span the cultural gap between biblical and modern times by expressing faith in categories with which contemporary people can resonate. Karl Rahner's *Foundations of Christian Faith*[42] is similarly motivated, although Rahner freely employs traditional categories of Catholic theology more than Küng. What is central to Rahner's hermeneutical approach is his insistence that theology must always talk about the depths of human existence. Through his use of what he calls "transcendental experience,"[43] he attempts to ground the essentials of Christian faith within the horizons of human self-understanding.

Hermeneutics, as it has taken on a wider reference, from explaining texts to understanding human experience, has come into the domain of thinkers outside of theology. Hans-Georg Gadamer in *Truth and Method* examines hermeneutics in this wider frame. Believing that the hermeneutical task should go beyond the scientific investigation of the text, Gadamer proposes that hermeneutics has to do with gaining truth and insight. He writes that hermeneutics is concerned to seek that experience of truth that transcends the sphere of the control of scientific method wherever it is to be found, and to inquire into its legitimacy.[44] Gadamer is not so much concerned with the methodology of the human sciences but with an attempt to understand why these human sciences are as they are and how they connect us with "the totality of our experience of the world."[45] What is of central importance in Gadamer's view is the way the interpreter encounters the tradition of the past through language in order to achieve understanding. By the "fusing of horizons,"[46] the horizon of the past with that of the interpreter, the interpreter develops an "effective-historical consciousness"[47] which enables understanding to take place.

Paul Ricoeur shares the view that the hermeneutical question is essentially the primary philosophical question. He focuses his concern, though, on another area, one which has become the overriding issue of philosophers in the twentieth century—the philosophy of language. "Man" is language, as Ricoeur and Heidegger are fond of saying. Ricoeur's interests range widely. He is not primarily concerned with the exposition of the Bible for the community of faith but with the rational clarification of human existence in the world.[48] He does, however, speak to the question of biblical hermeneutics. Lewis Mudge has outlined three dimensions to Ricoeur's philosophical hermeneutic as it applies to Scripture.[49]

The first he calls "Testimony in the Making" in which he describes the process by which a text becomes revelatory. It happens when the events of testimony are set down in discourse and by their own self-reference claim to be traces of the Absolute in a particular moment of history. The second dimension is the "Critical Moment," when it must be judged whether the text fulfills its claims. The question that arises, of course, is when does this happen, and in answering this question Ricoeur is not preoccupied with the traditional historical question of "whether it happened" but with hearing the language as it discloses being and allows the reader to project his or her possibilities. The third dimension, called by Mudge the "Post-Critical Moment," speaks to what happens when we receive a text as the word to us, making the testimony of the text our own. What it does is relieve us of our pretentions and move us toward "freedom in the light of hope," a concept not unlike that developed by Jürgen Moltmann.

Ricoeur's view develops over and against the psychological hermeneutic of Schleiermacher and Dilthey. He argues that Romanticist hermeneutics maintained an untenable dichotomy between understanding and explanation.[50] These two concepts should be kept in dialectical tension, a tension from which emerges the most constructive interpretation of a text. To understand the author's intention *(verstehen)* and the actual utterance *(erklären)* is a circular process. Explanation is possible because there is an autonomous process that "proceeds from the exteriorization of the event in the meaning, which is made complete by writing and the generative codes of literature."[51] Then understanding, which is more directed towards the intention of the discourse, and explanation, which is more directed towards the structure of the text, become the poles of the dialectical tension. At this point, the term *interpretation* may be introduced to describe the whole process of human consciousness which includes explanation and understanding.

The movement in the interpretive task is from initial understanding (a naïve grasp of the meaning of a text as a whole) to explanation (a study of the analytical structure of the text) to comprehension (a sophisticated mode of understanding). In the preliminary reading of the text understanding is a "guess," since the author's intention is beyond our reach. It is not possible to return to the alleged situation of the author in order to recover the meaning of the text. Step two, mediating between the two stages of understanding, represents the effort of validation. Using tools drawn from the structural schools of literary criticism, the interpreter attempts to disassemble and reassemble the text in order to "explain" it. At this stage the interpreter remains at a distance from the objective text. What emerges in stage three is a "sophisticated mode of understanding, supported by explanatory procedures,"[52] which can be fully appropriated or made one's own, ultimately the aim of all hermeneutics.[53]

It is not possible to adequately summarize the work of a Gadamer or Ricoeur in a paragraph or two, and it has not been our purpose to do so. The discussion is rather intended to point out how central hermeneutics has become to the quest of understanding life for all such thinkers. The emphasis of both Gadamer and Ricoeur on the theory of knowledge, the philosophy of language, and on human existence reminds us that what is at stake is more than the interpretation of an ancient text. It is the probing of the mysteries of ultimate reality.

Concluding Observations

What may be learned from this survey of contemporary hermeneutical options? In the first place some starting point, or preunderstanding, is always present in the interpretation process; great care must be exercised to avoid its distorting influence. Invariably, hermeneutics proceeds from some "horizon of understanding." There is a general agreement that some clearly articulated hermeneutical approach—a self-consciously chosen preunderstanding—is an essential ingredient in interpretation if understanding of the text is to be facilitated. Ricoeur might be considered an exception of this generalization with his concept of "distanciation," but even Ricoeur argues for an *openness* to the text which allows the interpreter to be enriched by receiving a new mode of being from the text itself.

More particularly, it has been suggested that certain qualities in the interpreter are necessary for a sound interpretation. For example, it is necessary to have empathy and rapport with the author of the historical document (e.g., Schleiermacher); one must be open and listening (e.g., Ebeling); one must have a living relation to the message of the text (e.g., Bultmann); and one should be aware that the task of hermeneutics is larger than explaining the text, but is a quest for the understanding of new modes of being (e.g., Gadamer and Ricoeur). In other words, the interpreter's preunderstanding must consist of an appropriate body of assumptions and attitudes if an accurate knowledge of the text is to be achieved.

Now the question is: is there a general preunderstanding that supplies the interpreter with the minimum prerequisite assumptions and attitudes? Is there a foundational preunderstanding within which a person must work to adequately interpret the Christian faith? We would again point to the biblical contention that it is faith which is this broad ideological and attitudinal frame of reference. The person of faith has a certain amount of ideological affinity with the authors of biblical records, sharing with them a common belief in the subject matter about which they speak—namely, God. The person of faith has a living relation to the message of the text in that there is the belief that that person stands in relationship to the One to whose word the text testifies. And the person of faith possesses (or should possess) an open and attentive attitude in relation to the message of the texts, believing that they somehow contain or point to the revelation of God. In short, faith as a body of particular assumptions and attitudes is the preunderstanding necessary for an adequate interpretation of the Christian faith.

This does not mean, however, that every person of faith will be a competent interpreter. Possession of faith is in no way a guarantee of sound interpretation. Certain other skills and training are required in addition to a healthy, vital faith. Nor is there any implication that all interpreters who have faith will come to the same conclusions. Faith is rather a minimum requirement within which a number of conclusions may be reached, depending on the interpreter's background, theological orientation, and ecclesiastical tradition.

There is one final concluding observation to make from this survey of contemporary hermeneutical options. Several of these thinkers have tended to de-emphasize history as it is commonly understood as the milieu of God's self-disclosure. The psychological hermeneutics of Schleiermacher and Dilthey, the existential hermeneutics of Bultmann and Ott, and the linguistic hermeneutics of Ebeling and Fuchs (and Gadamer and Ricoeur when they deal with the biblical literature) offer a less than significant place to history as the avenue along which God has been made known. Of course, these thinkers are concerned with history. Here it is more a question of emphasis. But the central message of the Bible—that God has been made known on the plane of history, and primarily so in Jesus Christ—should not be undercut. It follows that any hermeneutic which takes its cue from Scripture must deal not only with such issues as the interpreter's relationship to the text and linguistic study, but with the concept of God's self-disclosure in history as well.

SUGGESTED READING

Barr, James. *The Bible in the Modern World*. New York: Harper and Row, 1976.

Bernstein, Richard J. *Beyond Objectivism and Relativism: Science, Hermeneutics, and Praxis*. Philadelphia: University of Pennsylvania, 1983.

Gadamer, Hans-Georg. *Truth and Method*. New York: Seabury, 1975.

Klemm, David E. *The Hermeneutical Theory of Paul Ricoeur*. East Brunswick, NY: Associated University, 1983.

Palmer, Richard. *Hermeneutics*. Evanston, IL: Northwestern University, 1969.

Ricoeur, Paul. *Essays on Biblical Interpretation*. Philadelphia: Fortress, 1980.

———. *Interpretation Theory: Discourse and the Surplus of Meaning*. Fort Worth, TX: The Texas Christian University, 1976.

Robinson, James M., and John B. Cobb, Jr., eds. *The New Hermeneutic*. New York: Harper and Row, 1964.
Shapiro, Gary, and Alan Sica, eds. *Hermeneutics: Questions and Prospects*. Amherst: The University of Massachusetts, 1984.

10

A Brief Summary and a Modest Proposal

A Summary of the Argument

There is in the Apostle Paul a sense of incompleteness, of not having arrived at the shores of perfection or truth. The struggle is still very real. He writes,

> I consider that the sufferings of this present time are not worth comparing with the glory that is to be revealed to us. For the creation waits with eager longing for the revealing of the sons of God; for the creation was subjected to futility, not of its own will but by the will of him who subjected it in hope; because the creation itself will be set free from its bondage to decay and obtain the glorious liberty of the children of God. We know that the whole creation has been groaning in travail together until now; and not only the creation, but we ourselves, who have the first fruits of the Spirit, groan inwardly as we wait for adoption as sons, the redemption of our bodies. For in this hope we were saved. Now hope that is seen is not hope. For who hopes for what he sees? But if we hope for what we do not see, we wait for it with patience.
>
> (Rom. 8:18–25)

We do not see all of God's truth now; we wait patiently in hope for a clearer vision. In this present age, "we see in a mirror dimly, but then face to face. Now I know in part; then I shall understand fully, even as I have been fully understood" (1 Cor. 13:12). We know in part because we see from the perspective of our own limited vantage point. We read the signs of the world around us through our own particular set of assumptions and attitudes, assumptions and attitudes that we hold because of our total life situation.

Even Jesus saw the world around him and understood God from

the perspective of a first-century Jew, though his teachings certainly reflect a message filled with eternal truths. Yet he was born in an insignificant little province on the periphery of the Roman Empire. His name and family were Jewish, as were his Bible, worship, and prayers. He thought and taught in categories of first-century Judaism, proclaiming a message which could be understood, if not accepted, by his contemporaries. Maybe the freest and least limited of all human beings, yet even Jesus, *qua* human being, was bound by the language and customs of his age. He had no universal language with which to transcend culture, with which to think and express his thoughts about God.

His followers since that time to the present have been attempting to understand his life and words and translate his message into their own lives and words. In fact, the tasks of theology and proclamation are never finished, because each generation must interpret the faith in its own categories of understanding and relevance. Theology is not written once and for all, nor does one sermon speak with the same force to all eras, cultures, and ages. The church is in the business of continually sharing a partial truth—its perspective on God's self-disclosure. The interpreter of faith must begin the task with a single limited perspective.

This limited perspective has both a positive and negative role to play. The negative is obvious enough—when one allows preunderstandings to distort the interpretation. The positive role of preconceptions is less frequently recognized. It consists in the simple fact that we can apprehend *nothing at all* without some sort of prior structure. We would stare in incomprehension if we did not have some categories in which to "make sense" out of that which we observe. Indeed, different aspects of reality suggest, even demand, an appropriate corresponding prior structure present in the observer in order to be correctly grasped and interpreted. Assuming that the Christian faith is no exception to this general rule, finding the appropriate and receptive set of assumptions and attitudes is necessary to its comprehension also.

This argument is meant to advocate an "internalist" position, i.e., the position that the Christian faith should be interpreted partly in its own terms and from the perspective of an insider, as opposed to an "externalist" view which would endeavor to maintain distance and "objectivity." There is precedence for this proposal in Ricoeur's concept of a "second naïveté"; and in keeping with this internalist position, we contend that faith must be present if one is to move toward a full understanding of the Christian revelation. One has to see revelation and grasp it from within. It is the person of faith and only the person of faith who is open to the possibility that God is revealed in the domain of history.

One who has faith stands in a personal relationship to God. God is "known" through Jesus Christ. Christian truth is not only factual but personal also. The divine presence is known not just by the history of God's revelatory acts, but also by the incorporation of these acts into the contemporary life of the believer by the Holy Spirit. Christian claims are confirmed by God in the believer's experience, and it is the person of faith who has a sympathetic attitude toward the facts surrounding the appearance of Christ. The person of faith has sensitivity and insight that give her or him the capacity to appreciate and identify with the Christian message. There is affinity and rapport with the material to be interpreted.

This internalist emphasis upon faith must be balanced, though, by a recognition that faith itself assumes a cultural form. Faith looked on as a set of assumptions and attitudes takes shape in a particular historical era. This sort of faith is never free from the predominant thought forms of its time. Indeed, faith is only made meaningful when it is expressed in these thought forms. Although faith has certain universal constants, there are always constants which are inevitably and rightly conceptualized in terms of the external categories current in a particular cultural milieu.

Awareness of this point has led us to the second major strand of our theme, namely, the relationship of faith to history. Believing that there is no such thing as "pure" faith—faith free from cultural conditioning—we have argued that faith must be joined with the historical method in order to form an appropriate frame of reference for interpreting the Christian revelation. The historical method must serve as a means of filtering out the biases that inevitably accompany and distort faith. We have argued that it is only through the rigorous application of the historical method that faith is prevented from postulating whatever it wishes.

We have also maintained an even more basic reason for utilizing the historical method in the interpretive task—the Christian contention that God has been made known in history, and uniquely so in Jesus Christ. The interpretation of the Christian faith, because of its central affirmation of God's self-disclosure in Jesus Christ, is intimately bound up with the study of history. Two points are crucial here: (1) because the historian does not have direct access to the series of events that is being examined and because one cannot escape the influence of preconceptions, the resulting judgments have the character of probability, not absolute certainty; and (2) historical study need not necessarily be bound to any presupposition that precludes the possibility of postulating God as an active agent in history.

These conclusions clear the way for a discussion of the implications involved in subjecting the Christian faith to a historical examination. The sources available to us in the Christian faith (Scripture and tradition) must be subjected to a critical historical examination if we are to understand them and the faith about which they speak. Further, the historical study of the biblical manuscripts and the Christian tradition, together with an openness to the possibility that God could act in history (faith), leads to the point where one can affirm the probability that God has been revealed in the Christ event. Our conclusion is that faith and history constitute the minimum requirements for a hermeneutic that makes possible a "full understanding" of the Christian revelation.

The interpreter who comes to Scripture in faith and historical awareness generally brings certain assumptions about the nature of the Bible and how it functions within the life of the church. These critical assumptions about which the interpreter must be clear revolve around the way in which the Bible is seen as the locus of revelation, the carrier of God's word, and the authority for faith and practice. An analysis of these critical assumptions has led us directly into a discussion of an appropriate methodology for the study of the Bible. Our essential conclusion is that the Bible should be approached with all the resources that historical and linguistic scholarship make available.

But the utilization of a thoroughgoing historical-critical approach raises the question of how the Bible can still be preserved as the Scripture of the church. Our contention has been that the common testimony of the biblical authors to the redemptive love of God causes the Bible to function as the locus of revelation and as normative for the life and thought of the church.

We have also dealt with ways in which the interpreter might approach the many different kinds of literature that are in the Bible. Poetry and prophecy, history and theology, each needing principles and methods appropriate to its peculiar character and style. Guiding principles have been suggested for each genre as well as several general principles to assist the interpreter in relating one unit of Scripture to another. The "bottom line" once again yields the assertion of the central importance of history and faith as the minimum requirements for an adequate biblical hermeneutic.

The section of this book on the practice of hermeneutics within the church concluded with an analysis of the role which the Bible plays in the work of theology and the use of the Bible as a resource for ministry. Theology, as the church's reflection on God's self-disclosure, is rightly subject to the authority of the Bible in that the Bible alone witnesses to God's revelatory acts. In reverence to the Bible's use in ministry, we have maintained that in the hands of sensitive and caring people, the Bible serves the critical function of enabling individual Christians and the community of faith to move toward becoming all that God intends them to be.

In Section III a historical perspective on the subject of hermeneutics was introduced. Our purpose in doing so has been to test the validity of this argument in light of representative interpretations of the Bible which have appeared during the life of the church, to analyze these representative interpretations by the main contentions of our theme, and to discover by this analysis some guidelines for a constructive hermeneutical position.

We have noted that the Christian revelation is more apt to be seriously distorted when one of these elements essential to any adequate interpretation is missing. In the first instance, distortion occurs when faith is either not present or completely overshadowed by another point of view.

We have also observed the danger of distortion whenever there was either little understanding or neglect of the need to relate the Christian revelation to history. For example, Origen, because the ideas of history and historical study were as yet underdeveloped, was unable to appreciate the historical nature of revelation and to critically examine the historical sources.

The result of these studies is the continuing conviction that faith and history come together in Jesus Christ. This does not mean that all who have faith and join it with historical study will arrive at the same conclusions in interpreting the Christian faith. Our conclusion is still limited, and necessarily so, I think, by the perspective given to each of us by our age and our place in it. We will still make relative judgments which merely point to the absolute. On the other hand, these two guidelines do serve as a parameter within which a constructive hermeneutic can be framed for our contemporary situation.

A Modest Proposal

Finding a life-giving and rationally coherent faith in this present age is no small task. The world's overwhelming problems and the incredible amount of human suffering make one wonder where God is, or perhaps, even if God is at all. Even as one moves from unbelief to belief it is not easy to arrange the furniture of faith so that one can be comfortable with it. There are so many voices, so many competing traditions, so much within the Ark that does not ring true. But to give up or yield to cynicism is not a satisfying answer either. Surely, the way of faith offers more promise, though if we choose the path of faith it seems we are immediately forced into the hermeneutical question. How does what happened then make sense for me now? Where do I begin in piecing together a meaningful faith orientation that meets my spiritual needs and has integrity?

It is necessary to begin with the awareness that faith is pieced together from the experiences and exposures one has had. It is not possible to throw off the cultural conditioning of one's own time, to span the centuries and become a full-fledged citizen of the first-century Near East. We will bring to the interpretive task certain assumptions and attitudes which will take various forms and function in a variety of ways because of who we are. Some of these assumptions and attitudes may be consciously articulated and others may remain totally below the surface of explication. But we cannot escape them as we construct a coherent pattern of belief.

Because each of us inevitably peers at the givens in the Christian revelation through our own uniquely colored glasses, we need to maintain a good deal more humility about the positions we hold than is often exhibited. We should be aware that our formulations are only an approximation of the reality that we are attempting to describe. Our interpretation bears the stamp of a particular historical era, culture, tradition, and set of experiences. As we set about to put our views in some kind of order, we have an obligation to be conscious as far as possible of the particular contours of our preconceptions. This self-consciousness allows us to check and control the negative influences of our biases and accentuate that positive influence of our own distinctive point of view.

As we put forward our own views, we may take heart in the fact that even the biblical testimony to the Christ-event is cased in the thought-forms of the culture of the first century. To put the matter more positively, we know our responsibility is to formulate the Christian faith in a manner that our own generation can understand. This involves "translating" the biblical message into contemporary idiom and thereby employing concepts and categories external to the biblical material. The risk is that we will distort the essential message of the gospel by too much accommodation to the modern setting. But with careful scholarship, intellectual honesty, and a deep respect for the biblical witness to the Christ-event, the message can be reinterpreted for those of us who seek its life-giving sustenance.

To be aware of our limited vantage point is to be more open to other points of view and less defensive about our own. The Christian church has remained a powerful and vital force throughout history, in part because its universal message has been adaptable to so many different peoples and cultures. The church has a wealth of traditions in which to "cradle" the gospel, and the richness and depth of these traditions can inform our own. We are debtors to the lessons of church history and historical theology. They help remove the worst forms of our provincial and limited points of view and enable us to see the gospel in many new and vitalizing ways. We have two thousand years of teachers who have lived out their faith in different times and places to draw upon.

One fact, however, should not become lost in all this talk about relativism. There is a universal element for which we need not apologize. God has spoken in Jesus Christ, and the Scriptures bear witness to this gracious approach of God to the human family. Without this universal element, in fact, no reevaluation or reinterpretation would be possible at all. We lay hold of God's Word by faith, and faith, in its attempt to communicate Christianity to the present age must avoid an overaccommodation of the biblical message to the current mood. The present age may inform and rightly should inform our exegesis, but an interpretation that gives primacy to faith argues that the present age must ultimately be brought before the forum of the Christian message. Through such an interpretation Christ is made to speak; he presents himself to us in the pages of Scripture. Any viewpoint that attempts to find in Scripture only hints of eternal truths is an alien point of view to the Christian message. Yet this "faith hermeneutic" is always checked by historical study to prevent the unbridled reign of subjectivity. The historical method attempts to prevent faith from asserting its own historically conditioned distortions.

It is faith guided by historical study that supplies the clue to the interpretation of the Christian revelation. This minimal assertion certainly leaves a number of questions unanswered, but if they are to be answered, the solutions point the way to a possible hermeneutic for our time. One crucial question involves the way in which the actions of God in those unique revelatory deeds recorded in Scripture are related to God's actions in universal history. Two points, although hardly a full-fledged theology of history, suggest a direction to pursue in finding the answer. The first point is to remember that the God of the biblical witness is an active agent in tht totality of history. On the negative side this means the rejection of the position that God is active at some point of *kairos* and not at others, or that the presence of God in salvation history implies an absence of God in universal history. Secondly, remember that the God of biblical witness encounters and deals with the whole of history and the cosmos proleptically and prototypically through a special history, the history of the people of Israel and the Christ, in order to illumine the divine purpose and presence in and for the whole. The view that claims that the presence of God in universal history renders meaningless or useless the special action of God in the history of Israel and in Christ ultimately vitiates biblical faith. To bifurcate *Heilsgeschichte* and universal history as distinct theological alternatives is to misunderstand the biblical witness to the God who acts in the one for the many. Such a bifurcation implies either the absence of faith or the neglect of history.

A question we have thus far left partially unanswered here is whether there is sufficient historical data about the person of Jesus to form a basis from which to make the "leap of faith." Given all that has gone on in New Testament scholarship over the past fifty years, this question is a very real one. The answer should not take the form of an either/or—either the rejection of a historical view of the Bible or the denial that we can know anything about Jesus. Rather, the answer must be worked out in terms of a basic confidence in the historical-critical approach to unveil the essential elements of the life and person of Jesus. It is certainly not possible to recreate the life of Jesus complete with biographical chronology, topography, and psychological insight about his inner life. But it is possible on the basis of critical historical scholarship to outline the basic features of Jesus' proclamation, behavior, and fate. It is this information that is essential as a basis for the life of faith. History provides enough to give us the confidence to place our trust in God who has become known in Jesus Christ.

Another question which needs to be addressed is how Jesus Christ is to be understood in order to provide the pivotal hermeneutical principle for the interpretation of Scripture. Again without fully developing its implications, let me suggest this: an avenue of approach is to understand the guiding norm for the use of Scripture in the church as the inauguration of God's kingly rule in the resurrection of the crucified Jesus. This proposal could be expanded in three possible directions.

The first is to assert that the narratives about the life, ministry, teaching, death, and resurrection of Jesus assume a central role in enabling the Christian community to understand the particular way in which God's eschatological rule was inaugurated. These writings help to focus the rest of Scripture and enable the community of faith to understand what it is that God has intended for people across the centuries, an intention that is primary in the "story line" of the Bible. This assertion is not intended to imply that the biblical writings, particularly the Old Testament, should be read in an exclusively christocentric way, following Luther or Barth. It is rather to affirm that the coordinating theme of the Bible is the kingly rule of God which found its ultimate expression in the resurrection of Jesus Christ. To be sure, there are writings in the Bible which at best can only be construed to have an indirect relation to the theme of God's kingly rule (e.g., Ecclesiastes), but even these passages take on new meaning when placed in the context of the larger theme.

The second possible direction for expansion of this hermeneutic is toward the concept of hope. Believing that the Bible must be read with an eye toward the concerns of the present day and of the future, it follows that it is through hope that the desperate needs of the despairing world might be met; just as it is to hope that the kingly rule of Christ inaugurated in the resurrection of the crucified Jesus must point. Hope is the future now, the capacity to envision the future in such a way as to gain guidance and comfort in the present. The hope of the church is rooted in the belief that the God who raised the crucified Jesus from the dead is at work in the world today. The church's hope must be tempered by the subtle dialectic between crucifixion and resurrection, a dialectic which supplies the key to understanding the way in which God exercises divine power, and it is from this dialectic that the church finds its orientation toward mission.

This leads directly into a third possible direction for expanding the proposed hermeneutic. Scripture, as it is read with the theme of the inauguration of God's eschatological rule in mind, becomes the "marching orders" for the church's mission in the world. The God whose kingly rule was inaugurated in the resurrection of Jesus, an action that gives hope to the human family, calls the faithful to help accomplish the divine will and way in the world. God invites us to partnership in the creation of a more just and humane world.

It is Jesus who is the paradigm. It was Jesus who was fearless in attacking the hypocrisy and injustice of the religious and social system of his time. His words were a direct challenge to the oppressive political and economic structures that were characteristic of both the Roman and Jewish governments of his day. We should not be surprised that Jesus acted the way he did. His education, rooted in the Old Testament, could not help but create in his sensitive spirit and keen mind an uneasiness about empty religion and social injustice. He had read about Moses, the great champion of social protest, over and over again, the Moses who challenged Pharaoh and said, "Let my people go." He had read Isaiah and Jeremiah, prophets who lashed out against a religion which had no soul and a government which kept people in poverty. He had immersed himself in the writings of the later prophets, who spoke profoundly of the need for justice.

The purpose of God's kingly rule, epitomized in Jesus, is the liberation of all peoples. This is the message of the Bible. This is the mission of the church, which claims the resurrected Jesus as Lord, to challenge all forms of oppression and to help relieve human suffering in all its diabolical manifestations. God is not indifferent to the plight of the poor, the hungry, the illiterate, the victims of war and prejudice, and those oppressed by military, political, and economic tyranny. The church has no choice but to dive in and help those whose worldly address lies within one of the many suburbs of hell. It has no choice but to accept the partnership with God in the creation of a better world.

Notes

CHAPTER 1

1. Gerhard Ebeling, *Word and Faith,* trans. James W. Leitch (London: Fortress, 1963), 305ff.
2. James M. Robinson, "Hermeneutics Since Barth," *The New Hermeneutic,* ed. James M. Robinson and John B. Cobb, Jr. (New York: Harper and Row, 1964), 12–15.
3. Richard L. Rohrbaugh, *The Biblical Interpreter* (Philadelphia: Westminster, 1978), 29–35.
4. Carl Braaten, *History and Hermeneutics* (Philadelphia: Fortress, 1966), 131.
5. Ibid.
6. Robinson, "Hermeneutics Since Barth," *The New Hermeneutic,* ed. Robinson and Cobb, 19–20.
7. See M. Merleau-Ponty, *The Phenomenology of Perception,* trans. Colin Smith (London: Routledge and Kegan Paul, 1962) for a serious philosophical examination of this issue. See also Richard E. Palmer, *Hermeneutics* (Evanston, IL: Northwestern University, 1969).
8. C. S. Lewis, *Out of the Silent Planet* (London: Bodley Head, 1938), 38.
9. H. Richard Niebuhr, *The Meaning of Revelation* (New York: Macmillan, 1962), 10.
10. See, e.g., Carl Becker, *Everyman His Own Historian* (New York: F. S. Crofts, 1935), 233–255. See also Van A. Harvey, *The Historian and the Believer* (Toronto: Macmillan, 1969), 115.
11. Jacques Barzun and Henry F. Grant, *The Modern Researcher* (New York: Harcourt, Brace, and World, 1957), 160.
12. Immanuel Kant, *The Critique of Pure Reason,* trans. Norman Kemp Smith (London: Macmillan, 1962), 3.
13. Martin Heidegger, *Being and Time,* trans. John Macquarrie and E. Robinson (London: SCM, 1962), 144.
14. Magda King, *Heidegger's Philosophy* (New York: Macmillan, 1964), 8; italics mine.
15. Donald D. Evans, *The Logic of Self-Involvement* (London: SCM, 1963), 124f.
16. Ibid., 194.
17. Philipp Frank, *Philosophy of Science* (Englewood Cliffs, NJ: Prentice-Hall, 1957), 173.

18. Michael Polanyi, *The Study of Man* (London: Routledge and Kegan Paul, 1959), 27.
19. Michael Polanyi, *The Tacit Dimension* (London: Routledge and Kegan Paul, 1967), 20.
20. Michael Polanyi, *Personal Knowledge* (London: Routledge and Kegan Paul, 1958), 322–323.
21. Rudolf Bultmann, "The Problem of Hermeneutics," *Essays*, trans. James C. G. Grieg (London: SCM, 1955), 241.
22. Rudolf Bultmann, *Jesus Christ and Mythology* (New York: Scribner's, 1958), 48.
23. Rudolf Bultmann, *Existence and Faith*, ed. and trans. Schubert Ogden (London: Hodder and Stoughton, 1961), 289–296.
24. Günther Bornkamm, "The Theology of Rudolf Bultmann," *The Theology of Rudolf Bultmann*, ed. Charles W. Kegley (London: SCM, 1966), 7.
25. Alfred North Whitehead, *Science and the Modern World* (New York: Macmillan, 1927), ix.
26. John Macquarrie, *God-Talk* (London: SCM, 1967), 149.
27. James Barr, *Old and New in Interpretation* (London: SCM, 1966), 178.
28. David Elton Trueblood, *The Philosophy of Religion* (London: Rockliff, 1957), 54–56.
29. John McIntyre, *The Shape of Christology* (London: SCM, 1966), 16.
30. Ibid., 17.
31. See James W. Fowler, *Stages of Faith* (San Francisco: Harper and Row, 1981), 3–8.
32. John Hick, *Faith and Knowledge* (Ithaca, NY: Cornell University, 1957), 129.
33. Here a distinction can be made between faith (an integrating trust in God), belief (the holding of certain ideas), and religion (cumulative traditions). See Fowler, *Stages of Faith*, 9–15.
34. Hick, *Faith and Knowledge*, 196.

CHAPTER 2

1. See, e.g., James Barr, *The Bible in the Modern World* (New York: Harper and Row, 1973), 73–74, and James D. Smart, *The Strange Silence of the Bible in the Church* (Philadelphia: Westminster, 1970).
2. Milton S. Terry, *Biblical Hermeneutics* (New York: Phillips and Hunt, 1883), 18.
3. Karl Barth, *Church Dogmatics*, 4 vols. (Edinburgh: T. and T. Clark, 1958), III/1, 23ff. See also James D. Smart, *The Interpretation of Scripture* (Philadelphia: Westminster, 1961), 74.
4. Gerhard von Rad, *Old Testament Theology*, 2 vols., trans. D. M. G. Stalker (New York: Harper and Row, 1965), II, 319–335.

5. This view has been developed extensively by Walther Eichrodt, *Theology of the Old Testament,* 2 vols., trans J. A. Baker (Philadelphia: Westminster, 1961 and 1967).
6. See Brevard S. Childs, *Biblical Theology in Crisis* (Philadelphia: Westminster, 1970), 99ff., and James Barr, *Holy Scripture: Canon, Authority, Criticism* (Philadelphia: Westminster, 1983), 49–104. For an interesting discussion of the Old Testament and canonicity see Brevard S. Childs, *Introduction to the Old Testament as Scripture* (Philadelphia: Fortress, 1979), 41–106.
7. Ernst Käsemann, *Essays on New Testament Themes,* trans. W. J. Montague (London: SCM, 1964).
8. See David H. Kelsey, *The Uses of Scripture in Recent Theology* (Philadelphia: Fortress, 1975) and Dennis Nineham, *The Use and Abuse of the Bible* (London: Macmillan, 1976).
9. B. B. Warfield, *Revelation and Inspiration,* vol. 1 of 10, The Works of Benjamin B. Warfield (New York: Oxford University, 1927), 52.
10. A good summary of the debate may be found in Jack B. Rogers and Donald K. McKim, *The Authority and Interpretation of the Bible* (New York: Harper and Row, 1979).
11. Clark Pinnock, *Biblical Revelation: The Foundation of Christian Theology* (Chicago: Moody, 1971).
12. See Stephen T. Davis, *The Debate About the Bible* (Philadelphia: Westminster, 1977).
13. Ibid., 38.
14. See Karl Barth, *Church Dogmatics,* I/1, 98–140; I/2, 457–537.
15. See Barr, *The Bible in the Modern World,* 18–22.
16. J. K. S. Reid, *The Authority of Scripture* (New York: Harper and Brothers, 1957), 235.
17. See Hans W. Frei, *The Identity of Jesus Christ: The Hermeneutical Basis of Dogmatic Theology* (Philadelphia: Fortress, 1975).
18. See Hans Küng and Jürgen Moltmann, eds., *Conflicting Ways of Interpreting the Bible* (New York: Seabury, 1980).

CHAPTER 3

1. See Hans Küng, *On Being a Christian* (Garden City, NY: Doubleday, 1976), 145–165.
2. Thomas Aquinas, *Summa Contra Gentiles,* IV, 1, quoted by John Baillie, *The Idea of Revelation in Recent Thought* (London: Oxford University, 1956), 4.
3. See, e.g., Hans Küng, *The Structures of the Church* (London: Burns and Oates, 1964) and Karl Rahner, *Theological Investigations: More Recent Readings,* IV (London: Helison, 1967).
4. See Carl F. H. Henry, ed., *Revelation and the Bible* (Grand Rapids: Eerdmans, 1959); James I. Packer, *Fundamentalism and the Word of*

God (Grand Rapids: Eerdmans, 1958); Clark Pinnock, *Biblical Revelation: The Foundation of Christian Theology* (Chicago: Moody, 1971); and Harold Lindsell, *The Battle for the Bible* (Grand Rapids: Zondervan, 1976).

5. See Christian Hartlich, "Is Historical Criticism Out of Date?" *Conflicting Ways of Interpreting the Bible,* ed. Jürgen Moltmann and Hans Küng (New York: Seabury, 1980), 3–8.
6. Braaten, *History and Hermeneutics,* 12. See also Hendrikus Berkhof, *Christian Faith: An Introduction to the Study of the Faith* (Grand Rapids: Eerdmans, 1979), 45ff.
7. John McIntyre, *The Christian Doctrine of History* (Grand Rapids: Baker, 1957), 2.
8. David Kelsey, *The Use of Scripture in Recent Theology,* 64–75.
9. F. Gerald Downing, *Has Christianity a Revelation* (London: SCM, 1964). See also Dean Peerman, ed., *Frontline Theology* (London: SCM, 1967).
10. Alan Richardson, *History Sacred and Profane* (Philadelphia: Westminster, 1964), 65.
11. Reinhold Niebuhr, *Faith and History* (London: Nisbet and Company, 1949), 26.
12. Carl Braaten, *History and Hermeneutics,* 20.
13. Immanuel Kant, *Religion Within the Limits of Reason Alone* (New York: Harper and Row, 1960), 143, quoted by Braaten, *History and Hermeneutics,* 18.
14. Friedrich Schleiermacher, *The Christian Faith* (New York: Harper and Row, 1963), I, 49–50. See also B. A. Gerrish, *Schleiermacher and the Beginnings of Modern Theology* (Philadelphia: Fortress, 1984).
15. Schleiermacher, *The Christian Faith,* II, 478–480.
16. See Martin Kähler, *The So-Called Historical Jesus and the Historic, Biblical Christ* (Philadelphia: Fortress, 1964).
17. H. Richard Niebuhr, *The Meaning of Revelation* (New York: Macmillan, 1962), 7.
18. Søren Kierkegaard, *Philosophical Fragments,* trans. David Swanson (Princeton: Princeton University, 1936), iii.
19. Albert Schweitzer, *The Quest of the Historical Jesus* (New York: Macmillan, 1948).
20. Kierkegaard, *Philosophical Fragments,* 87.
21. Barth, *Church Dogmatics,* I/1, 188.
22. Ibid., 476.
23. Emil Brunner, *The Christian Doctrine of God,* trans. Olive Wyon (London: Lutterworth, 1949), 14.
24. Rudolf Bultmann, "A Reply to the Theses of J. Schniewind," *Kerygma and Myth,* ed. Hans-Werner Bartsch (New York: Harper and Row, 1961), 112.

25. Gerhard Ebeling, *Word and Faith,* 29.
26. Ibid., 204.
27. Barr, *Old and New in Interpretation,* 69.
28. Ibid., 67.
29. Wolfhart Pannenberg, ed., *Revelation as History* (New York: Macmillan, 1968).
30. Hans Küng, *The Christian Challenge* (Garden City, NY: Doubleday, 1979), 61.
31. Jürgen Moltmann, *The Future of Creation* (Philadelphia: Fortress, 1979), 59.
32. Helmut Thielicke, *The Evangelical Faith,* 3 vols. (Grand Rapids: Eerdmans, 1974), 209–210.
33. Karl Rahner, *Foundations of Christian Faith* (New York: Seabury, 1978), 142ff.
34. John B. Cobb, *Process Philosophy and Thought,* ed. Delwin Brown, Ralph E. James, Jr. and Gene Reeves (New York: Bobbs-Merrill, 1971), 382.
35. H. Richard Niebuhr, *The Meaning of Revelation,* 59.
36. George E. Ladd, *The New Testament and Criticism* (Grand Rapids: Eerdmans, 1967), 22.
37. Braaten, *History and Hermeneutics,* 36.
38. Heinrich Ott, "Rudolf Bultmann's Philosophy of History," *The Theology of Rudolf Bultmann,* ed. Kegley, 59.
39. Rudolf Bultmann, *History and Eschatology* (Edinburgh: University, 1957), 155.
40. Ebeling, *Word and Faith,* 37. See also Hans Küng, *On Being a Christian,* 157.
41. See Pannenberg, *Revelation as History.*
42. Wolfhart Pannenberg, "Heilsgeschehen und Geschichte," *Kerygma und Dogma* 5 (1959), 280; translation my own.
43. Ibid., 284.
44. For a full discussion, see James M. Robinson and John B. Cobb, Jr., eds., *Theology as History,* NEW FRONTIERS IN THEOLOGY, III (New York: Harper and Row, 1967). See also E. Frank Tupper, *The Theology of Wolfhart Pannenberg* (Philadelphia: Westminster, 1973).
45. For an interesting treatment, see Hugh Anderson, ed., *Jesus: Great Lives Observed* (Englewood Cliffs, NJ: Prentice-Hall, 1967). See also Gustaf Aulén, *Jesus in Contemporary Historical Research,* trans. Ingalill H. Hjelm (Philadelphia: Fortress, 1976).
46. Albert Schweitzer, *The Quest of the Historical Jesus,* 4.
47. See, e.g., Bultmann's article "Reply," in *The Theology of Rudolf Bultmann,* ed. Kegley, 274.
48. Joachim Jeremias, *The Problem of the Historical Jesus,* trans. Norman Perrin (Philadelphia: Fortress, 1964), 1.

49. Hugh Anderson, *Jesus and Christian Origins* (New York: Oxford University, 1964), 96. See also Eduard Schweizer, *Jesus* (Atlanta: John Knox, 1971).
50. McIntyre, *The Shape of Christology,* 41.
51. Stephen Neill, *The Interpretation of the New Testament* (London: Oxford University, 1964), 221.
52. Hendrikus Berkhof, *Christ and the Meaning of History* (London: SCM, 1968), 197. See also Leander E. Keck, *A Future for the Historical Jesus* (Nashville: Abingdon, 1971).
53. See James M. Robinson, *A New Quest of the Historical Jesus* (Naperville, IL: Alec R. Allenson, 1959).
54. Anderson, *Jesus and Christian Origins,* 97ff.
55. Günther Bornkamm, *Jesus of Nazareth* (New York: Harper and Row, 1956), 13–14.
56. Ibid., 24–25.
57. Ernst Fuchs, *Studies in the Historical Jesus,* trans. Andrew Scobie (London: SCM, 1964).
58. Ebeling, *Word and Faith,* 201–246.
59. Ibid., 204.
60. Ibid., 205.
61. John Macquarrie, *Studies in Christian Existentialism* (London: SCM, 1965), 148.
62. Richardson, *History Sacred and Profane,* 13.
63. See Willi Marxsen, *The Resurrection of Jesus of Nazareth* (Philadelphia: Fortress, 1970), 138–148.
64. Bultmann, *Kerygma and Myth,* 39.
65. See the list in Braaten, *History and Hermeneutics,* 92.
66. Pannenberg, "Heilsgeschehen und Geschichte," 266.
67. Jürgen Moltmann, *The Theology of Hope,* trans. James W. Leitch (New York: Harper and Row, 1967), 139–229.
68. Anderson, *Jesus and Christian Origins,* 189.
69. G. Bornkamm, *Jesus of Nazareth,* 180.
70. Richardson, *History Sacred and Profane,* 195.
71. Anderson, *Jesus and Christian Origins,* 185–240.
72. Richardson, *History Sacred and Profane,* 203.

CHAPTER 4

1. See, e.g., Brevard Childs, *Biblical Theology in Crisis,* 61–87.
2. See Carl F. H. Henry, *God, Revelation, and Authority* (Waco, TX: Word, 1979), III, 455ff.
3. See, e.g., A. Berkeley Mickelsen, *Interpreting the Bible* (Grand Rapids: Eerdmans, 1963).

4. See James Barr, *The Semantics of Biblical Language* (London: Oxford University, 1961) for a provocative discussion of this issue.
5. E.g., Gerhard Kittel, *Theological Dictionary of the New Testament,* ed. and trans. Geoffrey W. Bromiley, 10 vols. (Grand Rapids: Eerdmans, 1964–1976).
6. See Edgar Krentz, *The Historical Critical Method* (Philadelphia: Fortress, 1975).
7. See Raymond F. Collins, *Introduction to the New Testament* (Garden City, NY: Doubleday, 1983), 75ff.
8. For a good summary of the form critical method, see Rudolf Bultmann, *History of the Synoptic Tradition* (New York: Harper and Row, 1963).
9. See Norman Perrin, *What Is Redaction Criticism?* (Philadelphia: Fortress, 1969).
10. See Alfred M. Johnson, ed. and trans., *Structuralism and Biblical Hermeneutics* (Pittsburgh: Pickwick, 1979).
11. Paul Ricoeur, *The Conflict of Interpretations: Essays in Hermeneutics* (Evanston, IL: Northwestern University, 1974), 19–24.
12. Ibid., 13.
13. Collins, *Introduction to the New Testament,* 233.
14. See Barr, *Old and New in Interpretation,* 12.
15. I am using the concepts of "authority" and "normative influence" somewhat interchangeably.
16. See David H. Kelsey, "The Bible and Christian Theology," *Journal of the American Academy of Religion* 48 (1980), 386.
17. Ibid., 390–391.
18. Robert M. Grant with David Tracy, *A Short History of the Interpretation of the Bible,* 2nd ed. (Philadelphia: Fortress, 1984), 167–180.

CHAPTER 5

1. For a full discussion of the use of typology as an interpretive approach, see Smart, *The Interpretation of Scripture,* 93–133. See also von Rad, *Old Testament Theology,* II, 364–366.
2. I am indebted to Mickelsen, *Interpreting the Bible,* 179ff., for some of the categories in this section.
3. See Lewis B. Smedes, *Mere Morality* (Grand Rapids: Eerdmans, 1983) for a thoughtful discussion of the relevance of the commandments of the law.
4. Old Testament: Joshua, Judges, Ruth, 1 and 2 Samuel, 1 and 2 Kings, 1 and 2 Chronicles, Ezra, Nehemiah, Esther. New Testament: Matthew, Mark, Luke, John, Acts.
5. Other terms such as *legend* or *saga,* if carefully defined, may be useful.

CHAPTER 6

1. For a full examination of the question of the Bible's authority in the work of modern theology, see Kelsey, *The Uses of Scripture in Recent Theology,* 122ff.
2. See Paul Tillich, *Systematic Theology* (Chicago: University of Chicago, 1951), I, preface, vii–viii, 8. See also David Tracy, *Blessed Rage for Order* (New York: Seabury, 1978), 49ff.
3. See Hendrikus Berkhof, *Christian Faith* (Grand Rapids: Eerdmans, 1979).
4. See Gustavo Gutierrez, *A Theology of Liberation* (Maryknoll, NY: Orbis, 1973).
5. See Jürgen Moltmann, *Religion, Revolution and the Future* (New York: Scribner's, 1969).
6. See Horace Bushnell, *Christian Nurture* (Grand Rapids: Baker, 1979).
7. See Robert McAfee Brown, *Reading the Bible Through Third World Eyes* (Philadelphia: Westminster, 1984).
8. For an examination of this problem, see Richard L. Rohrbaugh, *The Biblical Interpreter,* 103ff.
9. See John R. W. Stott, *The Preacher's Portrait* (Grand Rapids: Eerdmans, 1961).
10. Ibid., 61.
11. See John A. Broadus, *On the Preparation and Delivery of Sermons* (New York: Harper and Row, 1944), 133.
12. See Barr, *The Bible in the Modern World,* 138ff.
13. See Dietrich Ritschl, *A Theology of Proclamation* (Richmond, VA: John Knox, 1960), 97–103.
14. See J. Stanley Glen, *The Recovery of the Teaching Ministry* (Philadelphia: Westminster, 1960), 99ff.
15. Wayne E. Oates, *The Bible in Pastoral Care* (Philadelphia: Westminster, 1953), 15ff.

CHAPTER 7

1. See Grant with Tracy, *A Short History* and Rogers and McKim, *The Authority and Interpretation of the Bible*.
2. Barth, *Church Dogmatics,* I/2, 727.
3. Küng, *On Being a Christian,* 165.
4. See Grant with Tracy, *A Short History,* 8–62.
5. Eugene De Faye, *Origen and His Work,* trans. Fred Rothwell (London: Allen and Unwin, 1926), 13–17.
6. William Fairweather, *Origen and Greek Patristic Theology* (Edinburgh: T. and T. Clark, 1901), 2.
7. Two excellent introductions to Origen's life and thought are Jean Danielou's *Origen,* trans. W. Mitchell (New York: Sheed and Ward, 1955)

and Joseph Wilson Trigg's *Origen: The Bible and Philosophy in the Third-century Church* (Atlanta: John Knox, 1983).

8. Eusebius writes that "when . . . the flame of persecution was kindled to a fierce blaze, and countless numbers were being wreathed with the crowns of martyrdom, Origen's soul was possessed with such a passion for martyrdom . . . that he was all eagerness to come to close quarters with danger, and to leap forward and rush into the conflict." *Ecclesiastical History,* trans. H. J. Lawlor and J. L. Oulton (London: SPCK, 1927), I. vi, 2.2.
9. Ibid., 3.12.
10. Ibid., 3.7.
11. Johannes Quasten, *The Ante-Nicene Literature After Irenaeus,* PATROLOGY, II, (Utrecht: Spectrum, 1953), 38.
12. Martin Marty, *A Short History of Christianity* (New York: World, 1973), 87.
13. Origen, *On First Principles,* trans. G. W. Butterworth (London: SPCK, 1936), p. 2.
14. Richard A. Norris, *God and World in Early Christian Theology* (New York: Seabury, 1965), 13.
15. Adolf von Harnack, *History of Dogma,* 7 vols., trans. Neil Buchanan (New York: Dover, 1961), II, 338.
16. Norris, *God and World,* 132ff.
17. Grant with Tracy, *A Short History,* 52ff.
18. Origen, *On First Principles,* I.3.1.
19. L. G. Patterson, *God and History in Early Christian Thought* (London: Adam and Charles Black, 1967), 48. See also Origen, *On First Principles,* IV.2.1—3.5.
20. Origen, *Selections from the Commentaries and Homilies of Origen,* ed. and trans. R. B. Tollinton (London: SPCK, 1929), 49, 50.
21. Origen, *On First Principles,* p. 8.
22. Arthur C. McGiffert, *A History of Christian Thought: Early and Eastern,* vol. I (New York: Scribner's, 1932), 212.
23. Norris, *God and World,* 139.
24. For a list of the difficulties which Origen discovers in the Bible see Frederic W. Farrar, *History of Interpretation* (London: Macmillan, 1886), 191.
25. For a discussion of this point, see Henry Chadwick, *Early Christian Thought and the Classical Tradition* (London: Oxford University, 1966), 112.
26. See Origen, *On First Principles,* IV.3.4.
27. One excellent treatment of Origen's allegorical methodology is R. C. P. Hanson, *Allegory and Event* (London: SCM, 1959).
28. Origen, *On First Principles,* IV.2.4.
29. Ibid., IV.3.5.

30. Origen, *Selections,* ed. Tollinton, 79ff.
31. Chadwick, *Early Christian Thought,* 157.
32. Origen, *On First Principles,* 8.
33. Both Augustine and Jerome were critical of Origen's views, and his teachings were officially condemned by the church in the sixth century.
34. See St. Paul's use of allegory in Galatians 4:24 and a discussion of allegory in its relationship to theological interpretation in James Barr, *Old and New in Interpretation,* 103–148.
35. See Origen, *Selections,* ed. Tollinton, xxviiiff. for a list of examples.

CHAPTER 8

1. One might argue for choosing Calvin instead of Luther to represent the Reformation and the modern era, and a good case can be made for Calvin. He was certainly one of the church's great exegetes, and his influence was profound, especially on the Reformed tradition. But Luther comes along first and sets a number of hermeneutical principles into motion, and I have, therefore, selected him to illustrate the beginning of the modern era in biblical interpretation. He has hardly been ignored. One biographer of Luther, Ewald N. Plass, in his *This Is Luther* (St. Louis: Concordia, 1948), 4, claims that more has been written concerning Luther than any other historical figure except Jesus of Nazareth. In addition to the various editions of Luther's works which have appeared, there are also excellent bibliographies available, many in the back of the better biographies. See, for example, Heinrich Bornkamm, *Luther in Mid-Career* (Philadelphia: Fortress, 1983); Mark Edwards and George Tavard, *Luther: A Reformer for the Churches* (New York: Paulist, 1983); George W. Forell, *Luther Legacy: An Introduction to Luther's Life and Thought Today* (Minneapolis: Augsburg, 1983); G. G. Haile, *Luther: An Experiment in Biography* (Garden City, NY: Doubleday, 1980); H. G. Koenigsberger, *Luther: A Profile* (New York: Hill and Wang, 1973); and John Todd, *Luther: A Life* (New York: Crossroads, 1983).
2. I am following the account given by Grant with Tracy, *A Short History,* 63–99.
3. Occasionally the number of meanings in a given text was thought to vary anywhere between two and seven, but four was by far the most common: (a) historical or literal which related the things said and done in the biblical record; (b) allegorical which deduced doctrine from the narratives; (c) anagogical which derived heavenly meanings from spiritual facts; and (d) tropological or moral which extracted lessons for life and conduct.
4. There are over two hundred biographies of Luther, many of them excellent. I have been helped by Roland Bainton, *Here I Stand* (New

York: Abingdon, 1950) and Robert H. Fife, *The Revolt of Martin Luther* (New York: Columbia University, 1957). The debates over this and that in Luther's life are endless. B. G. Rupp in his *The Righteousness of God* (London: Hodder and Stoughton, 1953), traces the historiography of Luther. See also Gerhard Ebeling, *Luther: An Introduction to His Thought,* trans. R. A. Wilson (Philadelphia: Fortress, 1970).

5. J. S. Whale, *The Protestant Tradition* (Cambridge: Cambridge University, 1960), 29–30.
6. See Heinrich Boehmer, *Der Junge Luther* (Stuttgart: R. F. Roehler Verlag, 1951), 41ff.
7. E. G. Schwiebert, *Luther and His Times* (St. Louis: Concordia, 1950), 150.
8. Ibid., 275ff.
9. Heinrich Bornkamm, *Luther's World of Thought,* trans. Martin H. Bertram (St. Louis: Concordia, 1958), 44–45.
10. Several volumes have explored the background of Luther's thought. See, e.g., H. Bornkamm, *Luther's World of Thought;* Schwiebert, *Luther and His Times;* Walter G. Tillmann, *The World and Men Around Martin Luther* (Minneapolis: Augsburg, 1969); and V. H. H. Green, *Luther and the Reformation* (London: B. T. Batsford, 1964).
11. Books which deal specifically with Luther's interpretation of the Bible are Gerhard Ebeling, *Evangelische Evangelienauslegung: Eine Untersuchung Luthers Hermeneutik* (Munich: Ch. Kaiser Verlag München, 1942); Michael Reu, *Luther and the Scriptures* (Columbus: Wartburg, 1944); J. K. S. Reid, *The Authority of Scripture* (London: Methuen, 1957); Sydney Carter, *The Reformers and Holy Scripture* (London: C. S. Thyrne and Jarvis, 1928); and G. S. Robbert, *Luther as Interpreter of Scripture* (St. Louis: Concordia, 1982).
12. Plass, *This Is Luther,* 49–50.
13. Though Luther could say: "Not only the words which the Holy Spirit and Scripture use are divine, but also the phrasing," in *What Luther Says: An Anthology,* ed. Ewald M. Plass (St. Louis: Concordia, 1959), I, 65.
14. Martin Luther, *The Table Talk of Martin Luther,* trans. and ed. William Hazlitt (London: H. G. Bohn, 1857), 12–14.
15. Plass, *What Luther Says,* I, 72.
16. Paul L. Lehmann, "The Reformer's Use of the Bible," *Theology Today* 3 (1946–47), 330–331.
17. Kurt Aland, "Luther as Exegete," *Expository Times* 69 (1957), 46.
18. Plass, *What Luther Says,* I, 91–92.
19. Martin Luther, *Luther's Works,* ed. J. Pelikan and D. E. Poellot (St. Louis: Concordia, 1958), XIV, 137ff.
20. Hazlitt, *Table Talk,* 4.

21. B. A. Gerrish, *Grace and Reason* (London: Oxford University, 1962), 143–144.
22. Farrar, *History of Interpretation,* 328.
23. Ibid., 327.
24. Plass, *What Luther Says,* I, 88.
25. Ebeling, *Word and Faith,* 306–307.
26. Plass, *What Luther Says,* I, 75.
27. Ibid., 94.
28. Ibid., 76.
29. Lehmann, "The Reformer's Use of the Bible," 337.

CHAPTER 9

1. Richard R. Niebuhr, *Schleiermacher on Christ and Religion* (London: SCM, 1965), 79. See also Hans W. Frei, *The Eclipse of Biblical Narrative: A Study in Eighteenth and Nineteenth Century Hermeneutics* (New Haven: Yale University, 1974), 290ff.
2. Friedrich E. D. Schleiermacher, *Hermeneutik, Nach den Handschriften,* ed. H. Kimmerle (Heidelberg: Universitatsverlag, 1959), 87. Schleiermacher writes: "Die Aufgabe ist auch so auszudrucken die Rede zuerst eben so gut und dann besser zu verstehen aus ihr Urheber."
3. Ibid., 109. "Die divinatorische ist die welche in dem man sich selbst gleichsam in den andern verwandelt, das individuelle unmittebar aufzufassen sucht."
4. See Niebuhr, *Schleiermacher on Christ and Religion,* 78.
5. H. A. Hodges, *Wilhelm Dilthey: An Introduction* (London: Routledge and Kegan Paul, 1949), 27.
6. Ibid., 114.
7. Wilhelm Dilthey, *Einleitung in die Geisteswissenschaften, Versuch einer Grundlegung für das Studium der Gesellschaft und der Geschichte,* GESAMMELTE SCHRIFTEN, vol. I (Stuttgart: B. G. Toubner, 1959), 375.
8. See Hans-Georg Gadamer, *Truth and Method* (New York: Seabury, 1975), 225–234.
9. Martin Heidegger, *Being and Time,* 147–150.
10. Macquarrie, *God-Talk,* 147ff.
11. Martin Heidegger, *An Introduction to Metaphysics,* trans. Ralph Manheim (New Haven: Yale University, 1959), 146.
12. See James M. Robinson and John B. Cobb, eds., *The Later Heidegger and Theology* (New York: Harper and Row, 1963), 14.
13. Macquarrie, *God-Talk,* 167.
14. Robinson, "Hermeneutics Since Barth," *The New Hermeneutic,* 38.
15. Ott, "Rudolf Bultmann's Philosophy of History," *The Theology of Rudolph Bultmann,* ed. Kegley, 55.
16. Rudolf Bultmann, "The Problem of Hermeneutics," 256.

17. Ibid., 259.
18. Ibid., 254.
19. Ibid., 255.
20. G. Bornkamm, "The Theology of Rudolf Bultmann," *The Theology of Rudolf Bultmann,* ed. Kegley, 10ff.
21. Gadamer, *Truth and Method,* 295–305.
22. John Dillenberger, "On Broadening the New Hermeneutic," *The New Hermeneutic,* ed. Robinson and Cobb, 148.
23. Ebeling, *Word and Faith,* 311.
24. Ibid., 313.
25. Ibid., 318. See also Gerhard Ebeling, "Word of God and Hermeneutic," *The New Hermeneutic,* ed. Robinson and Cobb, 93.
26. Ernst Fuchs, "The New Testament and the Hermeneutical Problem," *The New Hermeneutic,* ed. Robinson and Cobb, 141. See also Ernst Fuchs, *Hermeneutik* (Bad Cannstatt: R. Mullerschon Verlag, 1954), 126–134, 265–271.
27. Heinrich Ott, *Theology and Preaching,* trans. Harold Knight (London: Lutterworth, 1965).
28. Heinrich Ott, "What Is Systematic Theology?" *The Later Heidegger and Theology,* ed. Robinson and Cobb, 78–80.
29. Wolfhart Pannenberg, "The Crisis of the Scripture Principle in Protestant Theology," *Dialog* 2 (1963), 312.
30. Gadamer, *Truth and Method,* 269.
31. See Wolfhart Pannenberg, "Hermeneutik und Universalgeschichte," *Zeitschrift für Theologie und Kirche* 60 (1963), 90–121.
32. Pannenberg, "The Crisis of the Scripture Principle," 312.
33. Ibid., 313. See also E. Frank Tupper, *The Theology of Wolfhart Pannenberg,* 79–107.
34. See Jürgen Moltmann, *The Theology of Hope.*
35. Jürgen Moltmann, *Religion, Revolution, and the Future,* 83–107.
36. Ibid., 101.
37. J. Andrew Kirk, *Liberation Theology: An Evangelical View from the Third World* (Atlanta: John Knox, 1979), 35.
38. Gustavo Gutierrez, *A Theology of Liberation,* 6ff., 194ff.
39. For example, Charles Hartshorne, Schubert M. Ogden, John B. Cobb, Jr., Walter E. Stokes, S.J., Bernard E. Meland, Daniel Day Williams, Norman Pittenger, et. al.
40. See Delwin Brown, Ralph E. James, and Gene Reeve, eds., *Process Philosophy and Christian Thought,* 21.
41. Hans Küng, *On Being a Christian.*
42. Karl Rahner, *Foundations of Christian Faith.*
43. Ibid., 20.
44. Gadamer, *Truth and Method,* xii.
45. Ibid., xiii.

46. Ibid., 273.
47. Ibid., 274.
48. Paul Ricoeur, *The Conflict of Interpretations, 3–24.*
49. Paul Ricoeur, *Essays on Biblical Interpretation,* ed. Lewis S. Mudge (Philadelphia: Fortress, 1980), 17ff.
50. Paul Ricoeur, *Interpretation Theory: Discourse and the Surplus of Meaning* (Fort Worth, TX: Texas Christian University, 1976), 73.
51. Ibid., 74.
52. Ibid.
53. Ibid., 91–94.

Index